MW01702877

LIES MOMS BELIEVE

Praying that the Lord will use this book to encourage you in your mothering journey! ♥

John 8:32,

Rebekah Hargraves

Lies Moms Believe (And How the Gospel Refutes Them)

Copyright 2018 © Rebekah Hargraves

All rights reserved. This book or parts thereof may not be reproduced in any form, stored in any retrieval system, or transmitted in any form by any means—electronic, mechanical, photocopy, recording, or otherwise—without prior written permission of the publisher, except as provided by United States of America copyright law.

For permission requests, write to the author at: living_for_my_Lords_glory@hotmail.com or visit the author's website at www.hargraveshomeandhearth.com

Cover design: Kayla Nelson, Accidental Nomad Life Designs

Publishing and Design Services: MartinPublishingServices.com

ISBN: 978-1-7320818-0-2

All Scripture taken from the New King James Version®. Copyright © 1982 by Thomas Nelson. Used by permission. All rights reserved.

LIES MOMS BELIEVE

and how the Gospel refutes them

Rebekah Hargraves
of HargravesHomeandHearth.com

To the mama who daily finds herself battling lies
and the discouragement they bring.

This book is for you.

And to my own Mama, who put so much
work, dedication, thought, love, and effort into
raising and educating me. I wouldn't be who I am today
if it weren't for you. I love you!

"Her children rise up and call her blessed;"

—Proverbs 31:28

Motherhood Is a Woman's Highest Calling *Mothering Is Unimportant Work* My Identity Is to Be Found in Being a Mother *I Am to Find My Ultimate Fulfillment in Motherhood* Mommy Guilt Is Just Something I Have to Live With *It's Wrong for Me to Go to God Again and Again After I Fail* Theology Isn't for Moms *I Have to Be a Perfect Mom* I Have to Do it All *I Am Enough* My Children Would Be Better Off Having a Different Mom *I'm a Bad Mom* I'm Selfish If I Have Any "Me Time" *I Need a Lot of "Me Time"* Motherhood Has to Be Hard (And Hard Is Bad!) *I Have to "Keep My Act Together"* I Can't Have a Clean House While Raising Children *My Life Is Passing Me By* *I Am Responsible for My Child's Happiness* I Can't Do This Whole "Mothering Thing" *My Success as a Mom Is Directly Tied to How My Children Turn Out* I Don't Know What It Means to Be a Mom If I Only Have One Child *I Don't Have Time* My Postpartum Body Has to Look a Certain Way *Children Are a Nuisance and an Interruption* Children Are Really Expensive *Children Ruin a Marriage* My Focus Should Be on Rules and Regulations *The "Experts" Know Better How to Raise and Educate My Child Than I Do* The Most Important Thing Is My Child's Education *Good Moms Do "XYZ"* You Have to "Do" Motherhood the Way the Culture Tells You

Table of Contents

LMB

Battling the Lies, Finding Freedom

It all started way back in the Garden of Eden, this age-old ploy of Satan. It was the very tactic he first implemented in order that he might drive a wedge between God and Eve, and it is what Satan still uses today in his attempts to produce the very same outcome of division in our own relationships with God. What is that tactic, you ask?

It is getting God's people to believe a lie.

In Genesis, the Book of Beginnings, we read of how God created man and woman in His own image, charged them with the responsibility to faithfully rule over His creation, and then issued to them just one command: they were not to eat the fruit from the tree of the knowledge of good and evil. For, if they did, they would surely die (Genesis 2:17).

Then entered Satan.

Satan came along and, being nothing but a deceiver from the very beginning (John 8:44), craftily presented Eve with a lie designed to cause her to question God and His goodness towards her:

> Has God indeed said, 'You shall not eat of every tree of the garden'?" And the woman said to the serpent, "We may eat the fruit of the trees of the garden; but of the

> fruit of the tree which is in the midst of the garden, God has said, 'You shall not eat it, nor shall you touch it, lest you die.'" Then the serpent said to the woman, "You will not surely die. For God knows that in the day you eat of it your eyes will be opened, and you will be like God, knowing good and evil.
>
> —Genesis 3:1-5

Satan's end goal is always to lead people away from the Lord, and his primary method of accomplishing this is getting us to buy into lies—lies about God, ourselves, our families, and others. In fact, Jesus described Satan in these words:

> He was a murderer from the beginning, and does not stand in the truth, because there is no truth in him. When he speaks a lie, he speaks from his own resources, for he is a liar and the father of it.
>
> —John 8:44

Why is deception his chosen mode of operation in his mission to "steal, kill, and destroy" (John 10:10) us? Because he knows the Word of God to be true when it says:

> For as he thinks in his heart, so is he.
>
> —Proverbs 23:7

> Then, when desire has conceived, it gives birth to sin; and sin, when it is full-grown, brings forth death.
>
> —James 1:15

These passages show us the natural order of things. Rather than falling headlong into grievous sin overnight or suddenly one day deciding to turn our back on God, there is a certain order in which things occur that results in our being gradually drawn away from the Lord.

First, we believe a lie. It may even seem like a very innocent little lie at first. In fact, a lie like that is actually Satan's favorite kind—that sort of lie is easier for us to believe and embrace because it appears to be full of light and even contains bits of truth (see 2 Corinthians 11:14). Once the lie is then firmly planted in our minds, it leads to a desire of some kind as our worldview is slowly changed.

Second, desire then gives birth to sin, and sin brings forth death. Now, if we are children of God and have been redeemed by the blood of Christ, sin can no longer bring forth spiritual or eternal death for us. We have been saved from that. However, buying into lies and allowing those lies to bring forth sin in our lives can definitely result in the death of relationships, the death of peace, and the death of good works. It is a serious thing when we begin to believe one of Satan's lies because he knows the facts: believing lies affects everything, and a lie eventually leads to an action.

The Good News

There is great hope, however, dear mama! Do not allow Satan and his deceptions to fill you with fear, discouragement, or worry. As pervasive and powerful as Satan's lies can be, we have something far more powerful at our disposal with which to counter his lies: the mighty truth of God.

We are told repeatedly throughout Scripture that we are to take every thought captive (2 Corinthians 10:15), be transformed by the renewing of our minds (Romans 12:2), and gird ourselves with truth (Ephesians 6:14). That's what this book is all about—arming you with the arrows of discernment, wisdom, and Biblical truth that are required in order for you to easily recognize and combat the lies Satan likes to throw at you as a mom. He knows how very important your work of mothering is to the Kingdom of God, so he wants to wage war right there—at how you view motherhood, how you view yourself as a mom, how you view your children, how you view your parenting choices, and most definitely how you view God and the way He looks at you as a mom.

We know that it is the truth that sets us free (John 8:32), so it is my desire, through the writing of this book, to see you set free from the bondage of Satan's lies by the glorious truths of God's unchanging Word. I want to see you grow in your knowledge of the truth so that you might become thoroughly equipped (2 Timothy 3:16-17) for every instance of spiritual warfare in which you find yourself.

I have no desire to encourage you to go up against the lies you may be entertaining as moms by offering you my own thoughts or feelings—my opinions may help momentarily, but they would ultimately bring about no lasting change for you. Instead, I want to repeatedly point you back to the Word of God which is unchanging, alive and active, and sharper than any two-edged sword (Hebrews 4:12). Throughout the course of this book, I want to show you just how applicable the Word is to each and every lie you come up against, both in your own mind and in the world around you, all the while reminding you that just as Jesus intentionally used nothing but the truth of God's Word alone to combat the lies of Satan (Matthew 4:1-11), so should we.

So, what do you say? Let's get started!

How This Book is Set Up

As touched on above, this book is broken down into five particular areas in which Satan seeks to lie to us in our mothering: we will be addressing lies about the work of motherhood itself, lies about how God views us as moms, lies about ourselves as moms, lies about our children, and lies about our parenting choices.

If you have taken a cursory glance through the table of contents, you may have found that some of the lies in these lists appear to be different sides of the same coin or appear to be addressing different aspects of the same topic (e.g., the lie that "me time" is unimportant is then followed by the lie that you need a lot of "me time"). At first, the titles of some of these lies may seem a bit contradictory to each other, but that is because this is precisely how Satan works: he gets the people of God to believe in either the far left extreme or the far right extreme of whatever topic is at hand. Both sides, then, must be addressed.

It's precisely as one of my favorite writers and bloggers, Heidi St. John, says: "Satan doesn't care if he gets you in the ditch of legalism or the ditch of liberalism, as long as he can get you in a ditch." C.S. Lewis illustrated this point well when he wrote:

> I feel a strong desire to tell you–and I expect you feel a strong desire to tell me–which of these two errors is the worse. That is the devil getting at us. He always sends errors into the world in pairs–pairs of opposites. And he always encourages us to spend a lot of time thinking which is the worse. You see why, of course? He relies on your extra dislike of the one error to draw you gradually

> into the opposite one. But do not let us be fooled. We have to keep our eyes on the goal and go straight between both errors. We have no other concern than that with either of them.[1]

What is Meant by "Gospel" in the Subtitle of This Book

I have two definitions in mind for the reference I made to "the gospel" in the subtitle:

1. The first is what we usually think of when we hear the word gospel: that being the plan of salvation, the truth of what Christ accomplished for us on the cross, and the implications thereof (i.e. eternal life, a right standing before God, an imputation of the righteousness of Christ as our own, and a cleansing and forgiving of all sin and shame). This meaning of gospel comes through very clearly in certain portions of this book, such as when we cover topics pertaining to mommy guilt, feeling like we're "bad" moms, etc. The truth and beauty of the gospel as defined in this manner applies so very well to our everyday lives as moms, and I hope to make that clear as we go. Just as Laura Wifler and Emily Jensen of the Risen Motherhood podcast have inspired me to do, so I also want to inspire you to see how the gospel can—and truly does!—apply to every single little aspect of our daily lives as moms. From completing household chores to struggling with postpartum body image, we can take an aspect of the gospel, directly apply it to what we are dealing with, and watch it make a difference.

2. The second definition I am employing for "gospel" is the literal definition of the word: "good news". Under this much broader definition, I am referring to the totality of the Bible. In other words, in certain instances where we are discussing how the gospel refutes lies that we moms are believing, I will be referring to how God's Word, in general, refutes those lies.

With each lie we address in this book, we will be taking a look at what the lie is and what constitutes it as such. We will then proceed to look at how that lie is dangerous and could adversely affect our lives if we buy into it. Then, finally, we will discover the remedy to that falsehood and see how the truth of the Word of God addresses the issue. All of this will serve in equipping us to "not be conformed to this world, but be transformed by the renewing of your mind, that you may prove what is that good and acceptable and perfect will of God" (Romans 12:2).

Thank you!

Before we dive into the body of the book itself, I want to first issue a quick thank you to all the sweet ladies who submitted, via Instagram and Facebook, the specific lies that they have battled in motherhood. This book would not be what it is today were it not for their taking the time to share with me their experiences.

While I personally brainstormed several of the lies that made their way into this book as a result of having dealt with them myself, so many of the lies addressed in these pages were sent in by those other mamas. I'm so grateful this was the case because I truly believe that their input helped to make this book far more relevant than it would have otherwise been. After all, we are each affected differently by motherhood and by the lies Satan attempts to attach to it, for he cleverly hand-crafts particular lies for particular people. What was interesting, however, was that as I was going through and addressing each lie, the Lord taught me so much in the midst of my effort to teach others, and He revealed to me ways in which I had unknowingly been falling prey to some of those very same lies myself! God is so good in His desire to free us with His truth, and I am forever grateful for the work He has done in my own heart throughout the course of writing this book. It is my prayer that He does the same work in your heart as you read it.

God bless you, dear reader, and may this book serve to aid us in our work of:

> casting down arguments and every high thing that exalts itself against the knowledge of God, bringing every thought into captivity to the obedience of Christ... (2 Corinthians 10:5).

PART 1

Lies About Motherhood

Motherhood Is a Woman's Highest Calling *Mothering Is Unimportant Work* My Identity Is to Be Found in Being a Mother *I Am to Find My Ultimate Fulfillment in Motherhood* Mommy Guilt Is Just Something I Have to Live With *It's Wrong for Me to Go to God Again and Again After I Fail* Theology Isn't for Moms *I Have to Be a Perfect Mom* I Have to Do it All *I Am Enough* My Children Would Be Better Off Having a Different Mom *I'm a Bad Mom* I'm Selfish If I Have Any "Me Time" *I Need a Lot of "Me Time"* Motherhood Has to Be Hard (And Hard Is Bad!) *I Have to "Keep My Act Together"* I Can't Have a Clean House While Raising Children *My Life Is Passing Me By* *I Am Responsible for My Child's Happiness* I Can't Do This Whole "Mothering Thing" *My Success as a Mom Is Directly Tied to How My Children Turn Out* I Don't Know What It Means to Be a Mom If I Only Have One Child *I Don't Have Time* My Postpartum Body Has to Look a Certain Way *Children Are a Nuisance and an Interruption* Children Are Really Expensive *Children Ruin a Marriage* My Focus Should Be on Rules and Regulations *The "Experts" Know Better How to Raise and Educate My Child Than I Do* The Most Important Thing Is My Child's Education *Good Moms Do "XYZ"* You Have to "Do" Motherhood the Way the Culture Tells You

LIE #1

Motherhood is a Woman's Highest Calling

It may seem a bit counterintuitive to begin a book for moms by saying that it is not true that motherhood is a woman's highest calling. After all, this may not sound very encouraging for a mom to hear.

The most encouraging thing I could possibly do for you in your walk as a mom, however, is faithfully and consistently point you back to the truth of God's Word. And the Word of God never once refers to motherhood as being a woman's highest calling, nor does it hint at that myth.

In an effort to refute the lies of feminism which have pervaded our culture, conservative Christians have lately been proclaiming from the rooftops the sacredness and importance of motherhood, the reality that "the hand that rocks the cradle rules the world", and the belief that the work done by a mother at home with her children is of great eternal significance. At face value, there is nothing at all wrong with these sentiments—they serve to encourage mothers in their endeavor to successfully raise their children. I appreciate and wholeheartedly uphold these very truths myself, regularly writing on my blog about the beauty of motherhood and its grand implications.

However, we make a grave mistake when we take these truths about the sacredness of motherhood a step further and begin referring to motherhood as "a woman's highest calling". As important, beautiful, and impactful as motherhood may be, it is not a woman's ultimate role. When we mistakenly think it is, we end up inadvertently embracing some of the very same misconceptions that are held by the chauvinists of the world, who reduce the whole purpose of womanhood down to the bearing and rearing of children. In doing so, we end up taking our eyes off the Lord and His ultimate design for us as His followers.

Man's Chief End

One of the question and answer pairs contained in many Christian catechisms is as follows:

> Question: What is the chief end of man?
>
> Answer: Man's chief end is to glorify God and to enjoy Him forever.

We, of course, take this wording to refer to both men and women, and it is in this question and answer where we discover precisely what a woman's highest calling in life actually is. Though this concept from the catechism is not expressly found in the Scriptures word for word, several passages confirm its teaching to be true:

> Therefore, whether you eat or drink, or whatever you do, do all to the glory of God.
>
> —1 Corinthians 10:31

> Everyone who is called by My name, Whom I have created for My glory; I have formed him, yes, I have made him.
>
> —Isaiah 43:7

> You are my God; Save Your servant who trusts in You! I will praise You, O Lord my God, with all my heart, And I will glorify Your name forevermore.
>
> —Psalm 86:2, 11-12

> For you were bought at a price; therefore glorify God in your body and in your spirit, which are God's.
>
> —1 Corinthians 6:20

You see, our highest calling as Christian women is to glorify God with our lives as His servants. This is the ultimate purpose for which we were created. Here are a few other passages to illustrate this point:

> Now all things are of God, who has reconciled us to Himself through Jesus Christ, and has given us the ministry of reconciliation, ... Now then, we are ambassadors for Christ, as though God were pleading through us: we implore you on Christ's behalf, be reconciled to God.
>
> —2 Corinthians 5:18, 20

Finally, be strong in the Lord and in the strength of His might. Put on the full armor of God, so that you will be able to stand firm against the schemes of the devil.

—Ephesians 6:10-11

Be diligent to present yourself approved to God, a worker who does not need to be ashamed, rightly dividing the word of truth.

—2 Timothy 2:15

But you are a chosen generation, a royal priesthood, a holy nation, His own special people, that you may proclaim the praises of Him who called you out of darkness into His marvelous light;

—1 Peter 2:9

And Jesus came and spoke to them, saying, "All authority has been given to Me in heaven and on earth. Go therefore and make disciples of all the nations, baptizing them in the name of the Father and of the Son and of the Holy Spirit, teaching them to observe all things that I have commanded you; and lo, I am with you always, even to the end of the age." Amen.

—Matthew 28:18-20

> But sanctify the Lord God in your hearts, and always be ready to give a defense to everyone who asks you a reason for the hope that is in you, with meekness and fear.
>
> —1 Peter 3:15

> You are the salt of the earth; but if the salt loses its flavor, how shall it be seasoned? It is then good for nothing but to be thrown out and trampled underfoot by men. You are the light of the world. A city that is set on a hill cannot be hidden. Nor do they light a lamp and put it under a basket, but on a lampstand, and it gives light to all who are in the house. Let your light so shine before men, that they may see your good works and glorify your Father in heaven.
>
> —Matthew 5:13-16

> Do all things without complaining and disputing, that you may become blameless and harmless, children of God without fault in the midst of a crooked and perverse generation, among whom you shine as lights in the world.
>
> —Philippians 2:14-15

As evidenced by the passages we have just read, our highest calling as Christ-followers is to glorify the Lord in all we say, think, and do. This calling is then played out in our daily lives through our roles of pointing others to Him, evangelizing the world around us, living as salt and light, being about the work of reconciliation, working as ambassadors for Christ in the midst of a crooked and perverse generation in desperate need of Him, living as a picture of His love and grace to others, and faithfully living out the Great Commission as found in Matthew 28:18-20.

Why is it important to understand that motherhood is not a woman's highest calling, but rather that to be an ambassador for Christ actually is? The answer is five-fold:

1. When we say that motherhood is a woman's highest calling, what we are essentially saying is that all the childless women out there are "less-than". The implication is that they have not "arrived" yet, are not living up to the purpose God has for their lives, and must be of little use to His Kingdom, for they are not living out the "highest calling" for a woman's life.

   This is a tragic mistake, not to mention a very hurtful sentiment for women everywhere who may be barren, single, or struggling with miscarriage. To so reduce a woman's importance down to whether or not she is bearing and rearing children is an error detrimental to the very advancement of the Kingdom of God. Women were indeed created by God to be nurturing and caring in a special way typically not possessed by men. This does not mean, however, that women are found to be useful only if they put this nurturing side into practice with children of their own. Far from it! Women—whether single or married, mothers or childless—carry with them great influence and ability in reaching the lost and have an amazing impact on the world around them for the sake of the gospel.

   For example, due to our more nurturing natures, we women tend to be far more likely to gravitate towards showing love and grace than men typically are and can be powerful witnesses for

Christ in this way. We should not underestimate this aspect of our nature, but instead embrace and celebrate it as being the way God designed us. All women, whether mothers or not, are of great importance in the Kingdom of God and capable of much good, fruitful work for that Kingdom.

2. When we say that motherhood is a woman's highest calling, we are placing motherhood above our relationship with the Lord.

   In 1 Corinthians 7:34-35, Paul makes the statement that his preference would be for all singles to continue living the single life. He says, "There is a difference between a wife and a virgin. The unmarried woman cares about the things of the Lord, that she may be holy both in body and in spirit. But she who is married cares about the things of the world—how she may please her husband. And this I say for your own profit, not that I may put a leash on you, but for what is proper, and that you may serve the Lord without distraction."

   Paul is not saying here that marriage (or motherhood) is deplorable, nothing but a distraction, and to be avoided at all costs. After all, he goes on to say in Ephesians 5:22-33 that marriage is a tangible picture of Christ and the Church. He is, however, illustrating what our ultimate calling truly is: to care about the things of the Lord and to serve Him. If we are placing our children and our work as mothers over and above the Lord, viewing them as more important than our relationship with God, we are then essentially rendered unworthy of Christ (Matthew 10:37-38). This is a serious issue.

3. When we believe the lie that motherhood is a woman's highest calling, this leads to many of the other lies we will be addressing as we go further in this book.

Embracing the idea of motherhood as being a woman's highest calling—even if just subconsciously—leads to other lies that then have to be dealt with, as well. These include the lie that our identity is to be found in being a mother and the lie that we are to find our ultimate fulfillment in motherhood. Things go downhill from there, as these lies lead us to believe that if motherhood is supposedly a woman's highest calling, we must be a failure and a bad mom if our kids do something wrong or if we, at any time, have the desire to pursue any additional endeavors outside of mothering. We are addressing this lie first, then, because when motherhood becomes an idol, everything else gets off-kilter, as well.

4. This idea that motherhood is a woman's highest calling too often creates a dangerous and unhealthy desperation in single girls.

My friend, Nadia, made an excellent point on one of my Instagram posts the other day: "Teaching little girls that their highest calling is to be a wife and mama is part of why single, believing women struggle with discontentment when they reach adulthood, grow desperate, and sometimes 'settle'. Parents may be well-meaning but over-zealous in their efforts to counter the cultural disdain for motherhood; they're doing their precious little girls no favor by stressing that their purpose is limited to motherhood and wifehood." She went on to say, "I feel very passionate about this point because of how, somewhat painfully, it played out in my own life, causing spiritual turmoil, fractured relationships, and wondering for years. As a mother to my daughter, I pray so hard to know how the Lord desires for women to live and translate that into my life and actions."

Now, if I had read Nadia's wise words just a few short years ago, I would have balked at them. With indignation, as a result of some of the legalistic beliefs I held to at the time, I would have thought her to be wrong and to not understand the very purpose for which women were created, the high and holy callings given to them, or the sacred nature of marriage and motherhood. However, I have come to see in recent months that what Nadia is saying here is actually spot-on and a message we all need to hear. Are marriage and motherhood important? Yes! From the time I was a very little girl did I dream of nothing more than becoming a wife and mommy? Yes! Would I be OK with my daughter, Anna, having that exact same dream? Absolutely! If you are a wife and mom, is that to be your first and primary ministry? You bet! That is not, however, all there is to being a woman. Those are not the only two roles available to single women who are looking for something to do with their lives. "Wife" and "mom" are not the only two roles available to a woman desiring to live out Biblical womanhood.

Why is this important for those of us who are already wives and moms to understand? Precisely because we are wives and moms. What we believe regarding the nature of motherhood and the role of a mother is going to affect our day-to-day lives as moms as we will see throughout the rest of this book. In addition, as moms we are raising the next generation, directly impacting how they will view life and the choices they will be inspired to make. As Nadia shared, we as parents have such a lofty responsibility to train up our daughters well in this area of understanding what Biblical womanhood looks like. Because if we don't, the ramifications are huge.

The fact of the matter is that the idea of motherhood being a woman's highest calling actually contradicts Scripture.

According to God's Word, Biblical womanhood for Deborah looked like being a prophetess, judge in Israel, and leader in battle in place of the men who were unwilling to step up to the plate (Judges 4:4,9). For Ruth, it looked like gleaning in the fields in order to provide for herself and Naomi (Ruth 2:2-3). For the Proverbs 31 woman, it looked like prioritizing her husband and children while at the same time ministering to others and running a home-based business (Proverbs 31:10-31). For the female disciples, it looked like following Jesus and ministering to His needs (Luke 8:2-3). For Priscilla, it looked like running a house church (1 Corinthians 16:19) and a tent-making business (Acts 18:2-3) with her husband. For Lydia, it looked like running a business (Acts 16:14) and practicing hospitality (Acts 16:15).

Clearly, "Biblical womanhood" is about so much more than simply being a wife and mother (as if those roles weren't worthwhile and important enough!). Biblical womanhood is ultimately about serving the Lord first and foremost in whatever way He calls you. Even in the case of those of us who are wives and moms, our lives and exact callings will look different from one another. In my circle of local mom friends, I'm the only one running a blog, podcast, and writing ministry. I have one friend who is running a home-based business, while the majority of my other mom friends are all spending their time focusing on their families and living their lives as stay-at-home moms. And that is great! Each of these pursuits—online ministry, home business, and full-time stay-at-home mom—is just as valid and just as important as another because each one is a calling directly from the hand of God.

Why then is it important to understand (and to teach our daughters) the full picture of what Biblical womanhood is in God's eyes? Because to do otherwise—to believe and then to tell our daughters that their only choice in life is the role of wife and mom—oftentimes leads to the kind of unhealthy desperation Nadia talked about (and which I have seen myself).

When girls are raised to believe that they were made solely in order to be wives and moms (leaving no room whatever for any other calling God may have for them), and then they grow up and do not get married right away, a worry starts to seep in. A restlessness begins to fester. Questions begin bubbling up: *If my calling as a woman is to be a wife and mother, why am I not married yet? Where is my future husband? What am I supposed to do right now? How am I supposed to fulfill my purpose in life if I'm not getting married right away?* And then, the sad reality for many of those girls is that they fall prey to the handsome face of the first guy that comes along. They latch onto him in desperation, just sure that he is the answer to their questions—even if he doesn't love the Lord like they do or live in accordance with His Word. Things often go downhill from there.

The opposite response can also be true. Some girls, upon going through a few years of singleness following high school or college, can begin to grow bitter at not getting married and having children (or bitter that that was the only option given to them) and then forever disdain the beautiful roles of wife and mama. This is a serious problem.

When we take back marriage and motherhood from the legalistic camp and instead view them through the lens of God's Word, we will not say they constitute a woman's highest calling, but we will restore them to their rightful place as being beautiful, impactful, sacred roles for those women whom God has called to marry and have children. It's all a matter of perspective.

5. When we say that motherhood is a woman's highest calling, we make motherhood out to be the be-all and end-all. The whole purpose for motherhood and its very foundation are then lost, depriving it of its importance.

   The ironic thing is that when we claim motherhood is a woman's highest calling and make it an end in and of itself, we inadvertently separate motherhood from its whole God-given purpose. If we do not begin at the beginning and first understand our high calling and primary role in life to be that of ambassador for Christ, we as moms will lose sight of why motherhood is even important in the first place.

   If we do not believe our highest calling in life is our role of ambassador for Christ, and then view motherhood as an outworking of our calling to spread God's truth and make disciples, then what is it all for? What is the point of having children? Merely so that we would have someone to entertain us? When we instead begin to understand the role of motherhood in God's redemptive history, it is then—and only then—that motherhood obtains its full level of importance.

Motherhood in God's Redemptive Plan

In Genesis 3:15, we see the ultimate purpose for motherhood when God rebuked the serpent in the Garden of Eden by saying, "I will put enmity between you and the woman, and between your seed and her Seed; He shall bruise your head, and you shall bruise His heel." In 1 Timothy 2:15, Paul expounds on this promise: "Nevertheless she will be saved in childbearing if they continue in faith, love, and holiness, with self-control." It is through the avenue of motherhood that God chose to send His Son, the Savior, into the world. When we understand this, motherhood then takes on great value and importance! And while there was only one mother of that Seed and the rest of us moms are no Mary, motherhood nevertheless continues to be extremely important in our day, as well, for it is through motherhood and the bearing of children that the Lord continues His influence and impact in the world from one generation to the next.

Christian mothers are given the responsibility of raising their children to be disciples of Christ who will then, in turn, go into all the world themselves and further impact it for the Lord. To know this is to realize that the work of mothering is incredibly important! It is not, however, a woman's highest calling. Instead, in the lives of those women who have been given children, motherhood serves as a special and unique outworking of a woman's ultimate calling to be a glorifying ambassador for Christ.

May we keep first things first, sweet mamas. May we go throughout our days as Christian women reveling first in our highest calling to glorify God and spread His truth. Then, as moms, may we embrace the important role of mother with all that we are, understanding it to be our own special and unique way of fulfilling the Great Commission right where we are in this very season. May we, as women, keep our eyes fixed on Christ and, in so doing, fulfill our true highest calling each day of our lives.

Motherhood Is a Woman's Highest Calling *Mothering Is Unimportant Work* My Identity Is to Be Found in Being a Mother *I Am to Find My Ultimate Fulfillment in Motherhood* Mommy Guilt Is Just Something I Have to Live With *It's Wrong for Me to Go to God Again and Again After I Fail* Theology Isn't for Moms *I Have to Be a Perfect Mom* I Have to Do it All *I Am Enough* My Children Would Be Better Off Having a Different Mom *I'm a Bad Mom* I'm Selfish If I Have Any "Me Time" *I Need a Lot of "Me Time"* Motherhood Has to Be Hard (And Hard Is Bad!) *I Have to "Keep My Act Together"* I Can't Have a Clean House While Raising Children *My Life Is Passing Me By* *I Am Responsible for My Child's Happiness* I Can't Do This Whole "Mothering Thing" *My Success as a Mom Is Directly Tied to How My Children Turn Out* I Don't Know What It Means to Be a Mom If I Only Have One Child *I Don't Have Time* My Postpartum Body Has to Look a Certain Way *Children Are a Nuisance and an Interruption* Children Are Really Expensive *Children Ruin a Marriage* My Focus Should Be on Rules and Regulations *The "Experts" Know Better How to Raise and Educate My Child Than I Do* The Most Important Thing Is My Child's Education *Good Moms Do "XYZ"* You Have to "Do" Motherhood the Way the Culture Tells You

LIE #2

Mothering is Unimportant Work

As C.S. Lewis pointed out in the quote we read in the introduction, Satan's modus operandi for spreading deception is to present lies in pairs of opposites. And, it's a clever way of doing things. If Satan is unsuccessful in getting us to believe the lie on one side of the coin, then surely he'll be able to get us to believe the lie on the other, right? After all, it seems to refute the first lie, so it must be true. Such is the dangerous nature of deception. If we do not know the Word of God from cover to cover and have not been exercising our discernment muscles, we will be unable to spot lies when they come at us. We will be unable to "take every thought captive to the obedience of Christ" (2 Corinthians 10:5) because we will not even know what the obedience of Christ is.

The lie we have just looked at—that motherhood is a woman's highest calling—is used by Satan in conservative circles in an effort to distract Christians from understanding what the ultimate calling actually is for women (and men). The lie we turn to now is the one on the opposite side of the spectrum in this pair of lies, and that is the cultural idea seeping into the church today that mothering is unimportant work.

If Satan can't get us to believe that motherhood is the ultimate be-all and end-all for every woman (and thereby succeed in taking our eyes off our primary role as ambassador of Christ), then maybe he can weasel his way into our churches and homes by instead tempting us to avoid motherhood altogether—or to at least not fully embrace it if we are already moms—through the mistaken belief that mothering isn't a worthwhile endeavor.

When I reached out to ladies on Instagram and Facebook, asking them to share what the biggest lies are that they have struggled with in their mothering journeys, the responses I received revealed that many of them could relate to one another in having been deceived by this very lie.

> I've believed the lie that what I do as a mom really isn't all that important (but now I know this is kingdom work).
>
> —Marisa

> [I've believed] that our work as mothers and caretakers isn't good enough, and we need to do more and be more; when, [in reality], nurturing the hearts and minds of our children is a worthy way to spend our days.
>
> —Jenni

> [I've believed] that moms that choose to stay home and raise their own kids have no value, no drive, no ambition. 'Just a mom', I used to say, almost like it was an embarrassment not to have a career. The truth negates that lie--being a mom is the most important "job" I could ever have.
>
> —Vickie

It's a common lie precisely because of the very important nature of our work as moms—where Satan feels the most attacked is precisely where he strikes the hardest. He knows (better than we do sometimes!) that the work of mothering is kingdom work, so you can be certain he won't let it go unchecked.

The Great Commission and the Work of a Mom

One thing I love about our church is how each service is concluded by having the entire congregation recite the Great Commission mandate as found in Matthew 28:18-20:

> And Jesus came and spoke to them, saying, "All authority has been given to Me in heaven and on earth. Go therefore and make disciples of all the nations, baptizing them in the name of the Father and of the Son and of the Holy Spirit, teaching them to observe all things that I have commanded you; and lo, I am with you always, even to the end of the age."

I appreciate that this is the weekly practice of our church because each Sunday, as we embark on a new week ahead and all that it will entail, this recitation reminds us of what our mission and focus ought to be each day. For the mom, however, this passage can feel rather defeating and discouraging if we do not have a proper understanding of how we fit into this Great Commission.

For the mama who finds each of her days filled to the brim with changing diapers, nursing babies, answering never-ending calls of "Mama!!!", breaking up sibling squabbles, tending to toddler temper tantrums, wiping noses, making dinner, cleaning bathrooms, washing dishes, and perhaps seldom finding an opportunity to go to the bathroom alone, it can seem impossible to ever faithfully fulfill the calling of the Great Commission. I want to encourage you mamas with an important truth and that is this: you are already fulfilling the Great Commission right where you are when you faithfully go about the work of imparting God's truth to your children! Right where you are, within the four walls of your home surrounded by your children, you are daily obeying the commission issued to you by Christ when you train your children in the way that they should go (Proverbs 22:6). As you daily teach your children the Lord's commands, talking of them when you sit in your house, when you walk by the way, when you lie down, and when you rise up (see Deuteronomy 6:6-7), you are making disciples.

After all, your children are your disciples. They are your mission field. The Great Commission is all about teaching God's truths and commands to others, and what is raising your children up in the nurture and admonition of the Lord than precisely that? The point of the Great Commission is not so much the where, but the who and the what. Don't allow your focus to be on the fact that you may not be a foreign missionary daily spreading God's truth to people in the jungles of Africa or the urban cities of England. Yes, the Great Commission does speak of us going and making disciples of all nations, but I want to point out three things about that:

1. This wording is merely to make it clear to us that we are to leave no one out of the good news of the gospel.

   The command to "go out into all the world" illustrates that we are not to withhold the truth from Asians, but decide to share it with Europeans. We do not hide it from Arabs, but share it with Americans. God's truth is for everyone, everywhere! This does not mean, however, that you yourself have to go to one of those far off places as a foreign missionary in order to faithfully fulfill the Great Commission. After all,

2. In Acts 1:8, a passage whose message is similar to that of the Great Commission, Jesus says, "But you shall receive power when the Holy Spirit has come upon you; and you shall be witnesses to Me in Jerusalem, and in all Judea and Samaria, and to the end of the earth." Jesus speaks of His children spreading His Word to people both near and far, both in local cities and far off countries.

   Notice this: Christ never places one region of the world on a plane of more importance than another. There is no differentiation or partiality with Him. Again, God's truth is for everyone, everywhere. If you are being faithful—right where God has placed you—to share His Word with those in your particular circle of influence, then you are pleasing God and fulfilling the Great Commission just as much as the missionary on foreign soil.

3. Furthermore, in the passage from Acts 1, note that Jesus commanded His followers to be His witnesses in Jerusalem, in Judea and Samaria, and to the ends of the earth. This is worthy of pointing out because He proclaimed this message in Bethany, just two miles outside of Jerusalem.

   What Jesus was saying was that it is incredibly important to first faithfully proclaim the gospel right where you are, right where God has planted you. Too often we tend to romanticize the work done by foreign missionaries overseas and then fail to see the merit in the responsibility we have to proclaim the good news right where we are—in our own homes, neighborhoods, and communities. This responsibility is so important that, according to 1 Timothy 3 and Titus 1, it is faithfulness to proclaim the

> Word in the home and family first that is one of the important characteristics which qualifies people for further ministry in the church.

You see, sweet mama, you are already a missionary in Jesus' eyes! For some reason, we have made the mistake in our day and age of believing missionaries to be only those folks who serve people groups in foreign lands. However, a missionary is simply one who is commissioned to proclaim the gospel and to meet the needs of others, which makes you in your home just as much of a missionary as the dear folks serving others around the world.

But Am I Really Accomplishing Anything?

It can be easy for us moms to look at the great feats of faith and acts of service performed around the world by missionaries and evangelists and then look at our own day-to-day lives at home with our children and wonder, *Am I actually accomplishing anything? Yeah, I read the Bible to my kids, but mostly it seems like I'm just cleaning up messes and breaking up fights. How is this as worthwhile or important as serving others in impoverished nations?*

Oh, dear mama, let me try to encourage and inspire your heart today! It can be so easy to feel defeated and discouraged when we share God's truth with our kiddos and apply it to the issues of their daily lives, only for them to then act out and present themselves in public as little heathens. In those moments, we feel as if they will never get it, that nothing we are teaching them is actually sinking in. But let's remember the condition of our own hearts—many of us have been Christians for years, can spout off several Bible verses at the drop of a hat, and like to think of ourselves as believers and embracers of truth. But, in spite of this, how often do we sin and fall short again and again and again? Even the great Apostle Paul struggled with this! He said in Romans 7:15, "For what I will to do, that I do not practice; but what I hate, that I do." So, take heart when you see this happening in your children, too. It's not your fault or a sign that you are failing as a parent, for we moms are no different! It's all a part of the sin nature which still resides in us even after we are redeemed and washed clean (Romans 7:17-20). As you raise your children to be disciples of Christ, just remember what the Lord promises in Isaiah 55:11:

> So shall My word be that goes forth from My mouth; It shall not return to Me void, But it shall accomplish what I please, And it shall prosper in the thing for which I sent it.

Grow Where He Plants You

In all this talk of the Great Commission, I do not want you to be dismayed by the fact that you are not a foreign missionary doing great things in a far-off land. You need to understand that if the Lord wanted you to be a missionary on foreign soil, He would have called you to that work and sent you to that far-off land. If, however, for this season of your life at least, He has called you to live at home surrounded by your children day in, day out, *that* is the exact mission field He has in mind for you; that is where He wants you; those are the souls He wants you working to reach for His Kingdom. To do otherwise is to be in direct disobedience to His calling on your life in this season.

To forsake your God-given ministry to your children because you want a more glamorous or popular or public or seemingly more productive ministry out in the world is actually to forsake the Great Commission in your life. The Lord knew what He was doing when He entrusted your children to you, and He has called you to raise them for His glory and the advancement of His Kingdom. No other outside ministry could be more important or worthwhile or productive than that. Trust God and obey His call on your life. Lest you begin to think that to do so is to succumb to a life of smallness and insignificance, consider the encouragement and inspiration found in this quote:

> I alone cannot change the world, but I can cast a stone across the waters to create many ripples.
>
> —Author Unknown[2]

That, mama, is exactly what you are doing at home! Isn't that exciting? You are just one person and, even through the Lord, are only capable of so much. But when you pour your life into the lives of your little ones, you create ripples across the very pond of the world itself.

For example, do you have four kids? With just those four children, you are increasing your influence on the world four times over! You could be raising the next great political leader, an influential stay-at-home mom, the doctor who will cure cancer, and a pastor to be the next Johnathan Edwards, bringing about another Great Awakening. You never know what your kids will go on to do or how the Lord will use them, working in and through their lives. You simply know that He will, and you rest in that exciting truth, thankful to be able to take part in the amazing story He is unfolding in their lives and in the world at large. When you are faithful to do your part, you join the ranks of some pretty awesome moms:

> I cannot tell you how much I owe to the solemn word of my good mother.
>
> —Charles Haddon Spurgeon[4]

My mother was the most beautiful woman I ever saw. All I am I owe to my mother. I attribute all my success in life to the moral, intellectual and physical education I received from her.

—George Washington[3]

You are as much serving God in looking after your own children, and training them up in God's fear, and minding the house, and making your household a church for God, as you would be if you had been called to lead an army to battle for the Lord of hosts.

—Charles Haddon Spurgeon[5]

If I am Thy child, O God, it is because Thou gavest me such a mother.

—St. Augustine[6]

All that I am or ever hope to be, I owe to my angel mother.

—Abraham Lincoln[7]

Fulfilling the Great Commission with Your Children

Not only are you fulfilling the Great Commission as you raise your children to be disciples of Christ, but you can also emulate for them how they, too, can work to fulfill the Great Commission right along with you, side by side, as you "do life" together. The Great Commission is all about service—loving and showing one another grace and truth, meeting people's needs, and pointing them to Jesus so that they might, in turn, meet the needs of others. In this way the cycle of ministry and disciple-making is continued to the ends of the earth.

It can be so easy for me to sometimes want to be out "doing something"—serving meals at a homeless shelter, counseling teens at a crisis pregnancy center, or tending to a needy soul in some exciting way rather than sitting at home cleaning the kitchen or vacuuming the floor again. But do you know what? As my children grow, those areas of service will be something that I can do more and more (with my children right there beside me!). Will I also have other time-consuming parenting responsibilities (such as our choosing to homeschool) as our children grow? Of course! But an important part of homeschooling is not mere book work. It's life work! It is influencing, preparing, and equipping our children to make it their mission to love and serve others throughout the course of their lives. We need to begin viewing our families as a team whose mission it is to stand side by side and, together, impact the world for Christ.

As we instruct our children in the ways of the Lord, instilling truth into them and thereby fulfilling the Great Commission, we don't stop there. We then give them opportunities to actually put those truths into practice themselves by sharing those truths with others who are in need of the good news of Christ. We can take our children with us to the soup kitchen, the church visitation, or the crisis pregnancy center, fashioning them into little Great Commission workers, too! I love how Sally Clarkson so often speaks of how, when her children were young, she would not only read to them a great story of faith and heroism from the Old Testament or share an account of some great Christian in history who, by God's grace, did amazing things for His Kingdom; she would also go on to directly apply that story to the lives of her children by asking them, "What do you think the Lord can accomplish through you? What great thing could you do to advance the Kingdom of God? What great act of faith will you perform during your lifetime?" That's how I want to inspire my children!

As we all know, through the stories of people like David, Jeremiah, and Timothy, the Lord delights in using people who are young, who others would think incapable of great feats of faith. So, as we work to fulfill the Great Commission, let us not fail to inspire our kids to view themselves as Great Commission workers regardless of their age. Through the Lord, they, too, are capable of so much. The same Holy Spirit that the Lord gave to us to be our Helper is likewise in our children when they are saved.

So, mamas, live out your motherhood with purpose, joy, intentionality, a sense of possibility, and a heart for service, for you are a Great Commission worker right where you are with the family the Lord has given you. You are accomplishing great things in and through your home. Never forget that! Far from being "unimportant work", the work of mothering is world-changing work! You know what they say: "The hand that rocks the cradle rules the world." Satan knows this to be true. I hope you do, too.

A Word to the "Mundane" Parts of Life and Their Place in the Great Commission

As wives, moms, and homemakers, it can be so easy to sometimes feel like we are daily caught up in the mundane, feeling that all we ever do is wash dishes, tend to toddler temper tantrums, change diapers, reread the same picture book a hundred times, prepare meals, do laundry, break up sibling fights, and sweep floors, wondering what the point of it all is or if we are even accomplishing anything worthwhile with our time. We want to raise children who become godly, strong, gracious, fruitful, visionary adults, but we sometimes wonder what all these daily household chores and difficult "mundane" moments have to do with that end goal. We wonder if performing these tasks is even contributing to that goal at all.

Make no mistake—each of these tasks is important, and each one is serving as a building block for the kind of home you yearn to have and the kind of legacy you hope to shape. Each household chore you perform, each action you take of caring for the needs of your children, actually has a direct impact on your ability to fulfill the Great Commission in your home.

Though it is such a common catchphrase these days, I propose to you that there are no truly "mundane moments" when we are living with proper vision and a Biblical perspective. After all, the two main definitions of the word "mundane" are as follows:

- lacking interest or excitement; dull
- of this earthly world rather than a heavenly or spiritual one[8]

When we begin to understand that each and every one of the myriad little tasks we perform each day has a direct impact on the very futures of our children, we can certainly begin to find more "interest and excitement" in them, for we will see that they carry purpose, importance, and impact. So, that does away with the first definition!

Likewise, when we understand that our work within our homes is to be done "as unto the Lord" (Col. 3:23) and will greatly influence whether or not future generations within our care live for Him, we begin to understand that these seemingly "mundane" household tasks are actually not mundane at all, for they truly are spiritual, heavenly works, rather than mere earthly ones.

Though we have now successfully debunked the concept of "mundane" work, you may be left wondering how exactly our little daily tasks factor into the big picture of what we are wanting to accomplish in our homes as we raise our children. To answer this, we first have to grasp the fact that this day—and absolutely everything we do in it—truly is a building block for tomorrow and can be used to teach a valuable lesson.

When you have a newborn and are up at all hours of the night feeding the baby, changing the baby, rocking the baby, and calming and comforting the baby, you are building love, trust, intimacy, and relationship between you and that little one. This will serve as the foundation for the rest of that child's life and his or her understanding of what love, family, and home are all about. You are creating a bond which will serve you well the rest of your days as you seek to reach that child's heart for Christ.

When you have a toddler who stretches you in more ways than you could ever have imagined possible, and it feels as if your days are filled with little more than constant calls of "Mommy!!!", whining (on both the part of your toddler as well as yourself!), temper tantrums, and craziness, but in the midst of it all you still choose to shower that toddler with love, share cuddles, enjoy read-aloud time, have impromptu dance parties, and cultivate fun memories, you are laying yet another foundation in his life. It will be the foundation of your toddler's reciprocal love for you and his desire to obey and trust you and your parenting as he grows. Your toddler will have felt and seen, in a tangible way, your unconditional love for him.

When you kiss yet another boo-boo, you are instilling into the hearts of your little ones the knowledge that their mama loves them deeply, is always concerned about them and their well-being, hurts when they hurt, and is interested in what interests them.

When you do yet another load of laundry, you are working towards the health, hygiene, and cleanliness of your family—all of which are important, for with good health comes an increased ability to learn, work hard, live and love well, serve others, and advance God's Kingdom. Furthermore, as my husband pointed out to me, when our children see us performing our necessary daily tasks (such as laundry) with joy rather than with a grumbling, complaining spirit, this greatly influences them, as well. It helps to instill into our little ones an enjoyment of work which leads to a good work ethic. In fact, our daughter has grown so fond of doing the laundry that whenever I give her clothes to put into the washer or dryer, she excitedly snatches them away quick as a wink and says, in her cute little toddler voice, "Tank to, Mama!"

When you are cooking a meal, you are saying that you care about the nourishment (and the health) of your family. You are saying that you want them to experience the comfort of full bellies. You are extending love and life-changing, soul-enriching hospitality to whomever may consume that meal—family members and guests alike. Not to mention instilling a love for the culinary arts in your children!

When you read aloud to your little ones their favorite book yet again (even if it bores you to tears to do so), you are helping to instill in them a love of books and learning. You are cultivating in them a sense of curiosity and discovery, purpose and imagination, vision and excitement. For all you know, you could be raising the next C. S. Lewis, J. R. R. Tolkien, or Laura Ingalls Wilder!

When you are grocery shopping, you are again investing in the health and well-being of your family for generations, for the health of your children will affect that of your grandchildren, your great-grandchildren, and so on. You are presenting your little ones with a real-life picture of the Proverbs 31 woman who brought in her food from afar (vs. 14). You are providing your children with an understanding of what the best and most nourishing foods are. You are giving them a lesson in finances, good stewardship, self-control, and economics as you seek to: 1) find the best deals and 2) put your money towards the things that you need as opposed to the things that you want.

When you perform the grungy tasks of cleaning bathtubs and toilets, you are again investing in the health and well-being of your family, while at the same time instilling in your children the importance of these things. You are also providing your family and any guests who come into your home a warm, inviting, clean atmosphere in which to live, love, and learn about the Lord together.

We could go on, but I think you get the idea. The point is that everything you do within the four walls of your home can—and does!—have a great impact on your family and its future, not to mention on the hearts and souls of those folks to whom you extend hospitality. All of this matters for eternity!

In the New Testament, we find that much of Jesus' ministry, as well as the ministry of the early church, was conducted within homes among family, friends, and strangers alike. The home carries with it the potential for great power and influence for good when the maker of that home understands the purposes for which home was created. Lives can be changed, souls saved, and entire nations impacted for Christ when the homemaker grasps the exciting truth that nothing she does within her home is ever truly mundane. Every single thing she does has the potential to change lives, and, through her home, entire generations can be forever changed.

I hope you go forth today in encouragement and purpose, sweet sister! As you lay this book down and continue on with your tasks for the day, I hope you remember that the seemingly "mundane" work you are doing day in, day out in your home is not truly mundane at all—it actually carries great significance! It is important. It is life-changing, soul-redeeming, and heart-enriching. It is impactful. It is pleasing to God and a blessing to all who enter the four walls of your home.

So, what do you say? Let's remove "mundane" from our vocabularies once and for all! After all, as Gloria Furman has so aptly written:

> When the mundane looms larger than eternal life, we forget who God is, who we are, and who our children are. We tend to forget about tomorrow and eternity when our day is filled with the tyranny of the urgent. [9]
>
> When we have eternity in view, we respond to motherhood differently than if we lived just for the moment. We see that our children are marching toward a destiny. We consider that our temporary, fleeting struggles are passing away as we wait for Jesus, our blessed hope. We look forward to the day with anticipation of God's future grace, because our ordinary moments have meaning and eternal significance.[10]
>
> We need the compass of eternity to direct our perspective. It's easy to let our perspective get buried in an avalanche of cotton blends at Mount Laundry. Even so, we must make an effort to remember that our job is more than feeding, bathing, clothing, and facilitating education for our children. These tasks are meaningful in

and of themselves, because they're part of the stewardship God has given us. As Christian mothers God calls us to live with something we can only see with spiritual eyes—eternity.[11]

Motherhood Is a Woman's Highest Calling *Mothering Is Unimportant Work* My Identity Is to Be Found in Being a Mother *I Am to Find My Ultimate Fulfillment in Motherhood* Mommy Guilt Is Just Something I Have to Live With *It's Wrong for Me to Go to God Again and Again After I Fail* Theology Isn't for Moms *I Have to Be a Perfect Mom* I Have to Do it All *I Am Enough* My Children Would Be Better Off Having a Different Mom *I'm a Bad Mom* I'm Selfish If I Have Any "Me Time" *I Need a Lot of "Me Time"* Motherhood Has to Be Hard (And Hard Is Bad!) *I Have to "Keep My Act Together"* I Can't Have a Clean House While Raising Children *My Life Is Passing Me By* *I Am Responsible for My Child's Happiness* I Can't Do This Whole "Mothering Thing" *My Success as a Mom Is Directly Tied to How My Children Turn Out* I Don't Know What It Means to Be a Mom If I Only Have One Child *I Don't Have Time* My Postpartum Body Has to Look a Certain Way *Children Are a Nuisance and an Interruption* Children Are Really Expensive *Children Ruin a Marriage* My Focus Should Be on Rules and Regulations *The "Experts" Know Better How to Raise and Educate My Child Than I Do* The Most Important Thing Is My Child's Education *Good Moms Do "XYZ"* You Have to "Do" Motherhood the Way the Culture Tells You

LIE #3

My Identity is to be Found in Being a Mother

I would venture to say that this is a universal lie all moms have bought into at one time or another, perhaps even subconsciously so. In fact, a dear blogging friend of mine wrote in to say that the biggest lie she has believed as a mom has been this very one:

> [I have believed] that I'm 'just a mom.' Meaning, 'mom' was the only identity that I felt I had any more.
>
> —Kayla

Can you relate to that feeling? Perhaps you, like Kayla and I, have at times felt as if you are solely a mom, that the woman you were before you had children is forever lost to you. Or perhaps you have even found yourself believing that this is actually the way it is supposed to be—that once you become a mother, you are to identify solely as such, allowing motherhood to so completely drown out anything and everything else, that it leaves no room for the other interests, talents, pursuits, hobbies, or callings you may have had before becoming a mom.

Now, it is certainly true that we are to exercise a proper ordering of our priorities, being careful to live them out in a Biblical, God-honoring way. It is true that if the Lord has blessed us with children, then we are to dedicate much time and attention to faithfully bringing them up in the nurture and admonition of the Lord (Ephesians 6:4), training them in the way that they should go (Proverbs 22:6), and dedicating ourselves to viewing them not as interruptions to "more important work", but as blessings and rewards (Psalm 127:3-5). We should be looking on the daily work of motherhood as highly favored and important in the eyes of God.

However, motherhood was never intended by God to be our sole focus. As we have already seen, though motherhood is incredibly important and certainly a very high calling, it is not meant to be viewed as our highest calling, nor were we intended to "lose ourselves" in mothering, forgetting about the original woman God created us to be.

When it comes to how to properly understand our God-given identity and its characteristics, we should be viewing our identity in a manner as follows:

> First and foremost, I am a redeemed saint and Christ-follower.
>
> Second, I am a woman.
>
> Third, I am a wife, helper, and partner to my husband.
>
> Fourth, I am a mom.
>
> Last, I am a worker (whether at home or elsewhere), neighbor, friend, daughter, sister, ministry leader, and so on.

Do you see how far down the role of "mom" is on the list of the characteristics which make up your identity? This is not at all to say that the calling of motherhood is not vastly important (see lie #2 again). What it does mean, however, is that it is an improper ordering of priorities—

and, truly, a case of mistaken identity—to view our mothering as all there is to us, as if it were our sole or most important identity.

Let's turn to the Word of God to understand how this is true, to see how this mistaken identity is problematic, and to grasp anew what our true identity is thanks to the work of Christ on our behalf.

Who God Says You Are

I think we would all agree that it is who God—not ourselves, not Satan, not the culture, not even the church—says we are that is important.

You Are an Image Bearer of God Himself

It has oftentimes been said that woman was the crowning glory of creation, that after everything else was said and done, and the sun, moon, stars, plants, animals, and even man had already been created, creation was still incomplete until God made woman. We read in Genesis 1:27 that "God created man in His own image; in the image of God He created him; male and female He created them." This—being an image bearer of God—is the first identity assigned to women. As such, what we do in every other part of our lives should first be viewed as flowing out of the worth, dignity, and responsibility we carry as image bearers of the living God. All other roles we have must be viewed through the lens of the responsibility we have to first be faithful representations of Him.

You Are a Redeemed Saint in Christ

Throughout the New Testament, Christians are referred to as saints (Romans 1:7, Philippians 1:1, Revelation 14:12, 1 Corinthians 1:2 and

14:33), new creatures in Christ (2 Corinthians 5:17), redeemed (Luke 1:68), and a royal priesthood and chosen people (1 Peter 2:9). We will get into all of this more when addressing lies #5 and #6 about mommy guilt and coming to the Lord when we sin, but suffice it to say here that we are to base our identity on the solid, firm foundation of what Christ accomplished for us on the cross and live that out every day of our lives in whatever other roles the Lord has given us—wife, mom, homemaker, neighbor, etc.

The Problem with Finding Your Identity in Anything Other Than Christ

The reality is that when we place anything or anyone in the position only the Lord is meant to fill in our lives, our priorities become out of line and our ability to fulfill them is adversely affected. The fact of the matter is, Satan will do anything he can to take our eyes off Christ and our position in Him—even a seemingly-innocuous thing like primarily putting our eyes instead on our children and their needs, our duties as a mom, and the role of motherhood. Motherhood was never meant to become either an idol in our lives or the bane of our existence, both of which are far too prevalent views these days. Instead, for those called by God to be mothers, it was designed to be a beautiful outworking of the primary roles we were given to take dominion of the earth, be ministers of the Gospel, and live as image bearers of God and ambassadors of Christ.

When we forget the truth of this, we instead begin to base our identity on who we are and what we do, rather than on who Christ is and what He did for us. We look to our work and our accomplishments, forgetting His. The end result is that we live our lives in a way that shows we have inadvertently forgotten the very gospel itself and its implications in our lives. This can lead to a whole host of issues in our motherhood—

everything from making an idol out of it and placing it above everything else (including our relationship with God and our marriage), to producing an unhealthy co-dependency between us and our children which can stunt them in their growth to adulthood and rock your world to the core when they do leave home. It is a dangerous thing, with a whole host of ramifications, to find our worth or identity in any person or work other than Christ and His work on the cross.

Again, your identity, mama, is ultimately that you are a woman made in the image of God and a saint redeemed by Christ on the cross. Your identity is not found in what you do, but in Whose you are. When you understand both of these truths and walk in the freedom and fullness rendered you when you claim them as your identity, everything else will follow naturally from there. Jesus says in Matthew 6:33 that we are to "seek first the kingdom of God and His righteousness, and all these things shall be added to you."

When we do not lose ourselves or our identity in motherhood, but instead lose ourselves in Christ (Galatians 2:20), we are actually then—and only then—able to become better moms, for we will at that point be loving and serving our children out of the love and service we have been shown by Christ. We will no longer be wearing ourselves down to a pulp by doing nothing but tirelessly tending to our children, living out of a child-centric rather than a God-centric (and marriage-centric) home. Instead, we will be doing the important work of mothering out of the love, freedom, worth, and fullness we have found in Christ. And you know what? Our kids will be better for it!

Motherhood Is a Woman's Highest Calling *Mothering Is Unimportant Work* My Identity Is to Be Found in Being a Mother *I Am to Find My Ultimate Fulfillment in Motherhood* Mommy Guilt Is Just Something I Have to Live With *It's Wrong for Me to Go to God Again and Again After I Fail* Theology Isn't for Moms *I Have to Be a Perfect Mom* I Have to Do it All *I Am Enough* My Children Would Be Better Off Having a Different Mom *I'm a Bad Mom* I'm Selfish If I Have Any "Me Time" *I Need a Lot of "Me Time"* Motherhood Has to Be Hard (And Hard Is Bad!) *I Have to "Keep My Act Together"* I Can't Have a Clean House While Raising Children *My Life Is Passing Me By* *I Am Responsible for My Child's Happiness* I Can't Do This Whole "Mothering Thing" *My Success as a Mom Is Directly Tied to How My Children Turn Out* I Don't Know What It Means to Be a Mom If I Only Have One Child *I Don't Have Time* My Postpartum Body Has to Look a Certain Way *Children Are a Nuisance and an Interruption* Children Are Really Expensive *Children Ruin a Marriage* My Focus Should Be on Rules and Regulations *The "Experts" Know Better How to Raise and Educate My Child Than I Do* The Most Important Thing Is My Child's Education *Good Moms Do "XYZ"* You Have to "Do" Motherhood the Way the Culture Tells You

LIE #4

I Am to Find My Ultimate Fulfillment in Motherhood

Certain aspects of this lie are closely related to the lie we just addressed, but I wanted to deal with them separately. We just finished looking at the topic of our identity and worth from a spiritual, soul standpoint, and now we will turn things around just a bit and look at the physical, everyday life side of things.

It's a common myth, particularly in conservative Christian circles, that if you are a mother, you are to spend all your time focusing on your children, for "mothering is your highest calling" (here we see again why the first lie we addressed is such an issue—it really does lead to so many other lies!). Therefore, if you spend your time doing anything other than that work which in some way directly relates to mothering, then you may be in sin, or at the very least, guilty of misplaced priorities. This is false, plain and simple. I understand, however, how pervasive this mindset can be, having struggled with it myself on a regular basis.

Having been bombarded by the cultural lies of feminism for the past several decades, the conservative sector of the church has responded by running so far in the other direction that rather than landing squarely right smack dab in the middle of God's Word and His way of doing things, they have instead kept going until they landed all the way in far-right field in the legalistic camp. What began with a laudable intention—

the desire to reject the lies of feminism—has ended with the church using just as wrong of a thought process themselves as the culture does when embracing feminism. The only difference is which extreme the church is embracing.

This problem has resulted in a misunderstanding of what a woman's role actually is, what a mother is allowed to do with her time Biblically-speaking, what the responsibilities of a woman are, and what should constitute a woman's ultimate fulfillment. In a well-meaning effort to uphold the importance of the roles given uniquely to women (those of being wife, helpmeet, mother, and homemaker), we have been guilty of the idea that unless something you are doing with your time directly falls under one of those four headings, then you should not be doing it. More than that, some would say you may even be in sin if you do!

We have so fallen for this trap of wrong thinking that some Christian ladies are now under the impression that it is wrong for a wife and mother to earn an income or to pursue her passions and unique gifts in the midst of motherhood and homemaking. This unBiblical thought process again demonstrates precisely why we must know God's Word cover to cover, and why we must not fall into the trap of believing that motherhood is a woman's highest calling or that our identity is to be found in being a mom.

As we have already seen through refuting lies #1 and #3, our highest calling and our identity are based on who we are in Christ and our calling to be His ambassadors. This is also precisely where our ultimate fulfillment is to be found, as well. Just as it is wrong to believe that our husband is to fulfill or complete us, so it is likewise wrong to believe that our children and our motherhood are to ultimately fulfill or complete us. When we place anyone or anything in the position only God was meant to fill, we are guilty of setting up idols in our hearts and will face the unintended consequences of doing so. Perhaps you have witnessed one or more of the following in yourself or someone you know:

- excessive anxiety or worry in motherhood
- a co-dependent relationship with your children
- excessive "helicopter" parenting
- not being able to imagine life without your children in your home and feeling overwhelming sadness, depression, or a sense of lostness at the thought of having an empty nest one day
- excessive pride over your children's accomplishments or despair over their failures
- practicing no self-care in motherhood
- the belief that you must be with your children every moment of every day or else you are failing in your role as a mother
- the idea that you cannot take time to read, study God's Word, pray, learn, pursue your hobbies, practice and use your own unique gifts and abilities, or serve in the church if you are a busy mama or have young children (or, at the very least, will be weighed down by mommy guilt if you do!)

If any of these describe you at all, you have most likely made motherhood into an idol in your heart, allowing it to take up residence in a place it was never meant to fill. You are seeking your ultimate fulfillment in motherhood instead of first and foremost in God. This can be so easy to do, especially if you—like me—only ever dreamed of being a mama.

Again, while motherhood no doubt is so very beautiful and significant and needs to take back its level of importance that has been stolen by the culture, it nevertheless needs to give back some of the importance it has been assigned by the church to the One who designed it in the first place.

The idea that you are supposed to find your ultimate fulfillment in motherhood is a lie not only because your ultimate fulfillment is to instead be found in God alone, but also because that idea implies that the work you do as a mother is all you are allowed to do in this season of your life. We briefly touched on this concept above when I mentioned how the church is sometimes guilty of portraying mothers earning incomes or pursuing their passions as being in sin. Believe it or not, there are other things we can do while we are mothers besides just the day-to-day work of mothering—not in some ultra-radical feministic way that says you can go off and find yourself, give your children to someone else to raise, see them every once in a while, and pursue your passions to the detriment of your children. As with all things, there has to be balance and a right ordering of priorities. But to say that a mother can only ever be about the work of mothering and finding her fulfillment solely in that work is a completely unBiblical concept.

Motherhood in the Bible

Where we as the church commonly get ourselves into trouble with areas of wrong thinking (which lead to wrong living) is when we take church tradition, cultural norms or ideals, man-made expectations, or our own desires and superimpose them onto the Word of God, allowing all of those various mindsets and belief systems to color our interpretation of the text. This is precisely how Satan gets to us with all the lies we are addressing in this book.

If we, instead, as my dad so wisely says, allowed "Scripture to interpret Scripture", practiced the concept of Sola Scriptura (Scripture alone), and based all of our thoughts, opinions, dreams, decisions, methods, and ways of life squarely on what the Word says, everything about our motherhood would change for the better. Our families would be stronger, more joyful, more productive, and far more impactful for the Kingdom of God. In an effort to further refute the lie we are addressing, let's turn now to the Word of God to see what motherhood looks like, Biblically-speaking.

The Proverbs 31 Woman

This lady oftentimes gets a bad rap, which is terribly unfortunate. Here God has provided us with a clear and beautiful blueprint by which to pattern our lives as women. But instead of seeing it as such, we balk at her various characteristics and shirk away from the different roles and responsibilities we see her performing. In so doing, we fail to get to the heart of the matter—that being the general picture we have here of a woman who worked hard; was productive; who used her brain, gifts, and talents; who loved her family well; who faithfully met the needs of her household; who rejoiced in serving others; and ultimately, who feared the Lord and sought to please Him in everything. That's what this picture is all about—not whether or not you can sew tapestry.

What's interesting about this portrait of Biblical womanhood by God's design is that it directly flies in the face of the legalistic "moms-shall-not-do-xyz" mentality. Here you have a woman who so clearly had her priorities straight, for she feared God first and foremost (vs. 30), was a trustworthy wife and helpmeet, daily doing her husband good (vs. 10-12), loved her children with all her heart and faithfully went about the work of raising them well (vs. 27-28), and served others with helpful acts and financial assistance (vs. 20) and kind words of wisdom (vs. 26). She didn't stop there, however, nor was she commanded by God to do so.

She also was quite an industrious businesswoman and seamstress, producing beautiful garments and sashes and providing them wholesale to the merchants (vs. 24). Beyond that, she was also knowledgeable in financial matters and understood issues pertaining to real estate, having wisely considered what would be the proper field to purchase and put to use as a vineyard (vs. 16). While she undoubtedly was careful to first ensure that her priorities were in proper order and that she was not guilty of neglecting her husband, children, and household, the Proverbs 31 woman also ran a home-based business, completed service projects, and ministered to others. So, too, can we.

The Women Who Followed Jesus

When we understand that Jesus lived in a time when women were believed to be second-class citizens (or worse), told that they should not even be taught the Torah, and raised to believe that motherhood was a woman's highest calling (thus producing the feeling that we find women experiencing in the Old Testament of being utter failures and "less than" if found to be infertile), Luke 8:1-3 stands out as a most interesting little passage:

> Now it came to pass, afterward, that He went through every city and village, preaching and bringing the glad tidings of the kingdom of God. And the twelve were with Him, and certain women who had been healed of evil spirits and infirmities—Mary called Magdalene, out of whom had come seven demons, and Joanna the wife of Chuza, Herod's steward, and Susanna, and many others who provided for Him from their substance.

Now, what exactly is so interesting about this? It is the very fact that, in addition to the twelve disciples who followed Jesus from town to town throughout his three years of ministry, many women were in His traveling band of followers, as well—many of whom were most likely wives and mothers and, as such, would have been viewed as needing to be at home 24/7. Instead of legalistically shaming these women into believing that they couldn't follow after or provide for Him because of their roles, they were actually welcomed into His group of traveling disciples. This is such a fascinating realization, particularly when we realize that if they were married (as we know at least Joanna was), they may have gone out alone to do this without their families even being able to travel with them. Joanna's husband, for example, would have had to remain behind as Herod's steward, which means their children may or may not have been traveling with her, either.

As a conservative Christian woman who is passionate about Biblical womanhood, the God-given roles of women, and exposing the issues associated with feminism, I momentarily balk at the realization that these women may very well have briefly left their husbands and children behind to go and follow Jesus, serving Him along the way. This is precisely why it is so crucially important to know the Word of God cover to cover so that we do not fall prey to cultural or even "Christian" concepts as to what constitutes Biblical womanhood. We have to go straight to the source, the Word of God itself, allowing it alone to shape our view of ourselves as women, our roles, and our responsibilities. When we do so, we see that wives and moms are to faithfully love and serve their families first (second only to God, of course), being careful not to neglect them or allow other pursuits to crowd them out or to take precedence. Beyond that, however, women are given great freedom to pursue their unique God-given callings, dreams, passions, and interests in addition to the work of homemaking and motherhood. This is clear throughout Scripture.

A Word to the Mom Who Wants Nothing More Than to Pursue Motherhood

I do want to speak a moment to the dear mama who may be reading this and thinking to herself, *All I have ever wanted to do is be a mom. I don't have any desire to run a home business or launch a ministry. I just want to be a stay-at-home mom.* To that I say, "Go for it, sister!" What we have talked about in regards to the Proverbs 31 woman and the women who followed Jesus is not meant to make you believe that you have to have other pursuits beyond mothering and homemaking. Tending to the needs of your family may be precisely what the Lord has called you to in this season, and that, in and of itself, is highly important work. There is no shame in that whatsoever.

Therefore, our study of women in the Bible is not meant to "guilt you" into pursuing "more" with your life. Rather, it is meant to free women reading this who may be in the bonds of legalism and feeling called by God to pursue other endeavors (in addition to mothering and homemaking) and wondering if it is acceptable to do so. The bottom line is this: do what you know God is calling you to do, and rest in the joy of knowing that you are obeying Him and bringing Him glory in your everyday life.

To Sum It All Up

When it comes to the lie that mothers are to find their ultimate fulfillment solely in motherhood, we have to remember two very important things:

The first is that, ultimately, our fulfillment should be found not in motherhood, but in God Himself—in worshipping, obeying, and glorifying Him, living daily as His ambassador, image-bearer, and minister of the gospel.

Second, note the definition of "fulfillment"—"satisfaction or happiness as a result of fully developing one's abilities, potential, or character"[12]. For some women (such as myself) motherhood (as beautiful, important, and worthy of our time and attention as it is!) does not completely meet that definition of fulfillment for us. And that's OK. We know, according to 1 Corinthians 12, that all members of the body of Christ (including moms!) have been given unique spiritual gifts which He expects us to put to use for the benefit of the Kingdom. Now, should we be careful to exercise these spiritual gifts in such a manner so as to not neglect the needs of our husbands, children, and homes? Most definitely! As my friend Erika said during a podcast episode we did together, "Don't add another thing on to your plate, such as a business, unless you are already managing well the things currently on your plate."[13] We would also do well to remember that the spiritual gifts God has given us can be used specifically within the context of home and family. It is a fallacy, however, to automatically assume that if a woman is pursuing any endeavors outside the realm of homemaking and mothering, she must be guilty of neglecting her family. If we believe that, we need to take it up with the Lord because He included Proverbs 31 and Luke 8 in His Word for a reason!

When we remember the first point—that we are ultimately to find our fulfillment in being ambassadors of Christ—everything else flows naturally from there just as Christ promised it would in Matthew 6! We are then able to use our God-given gifts and talents in addition to taking good care of our families. That is precisely where the sweet spot is, where we will feel the sense of fulfillment in our lives that we were meant to experience.

Motherhood Is a Woman's Highest Calling *Mothering Is Unimportant Work* My Identity Is to Be Found in Being a Mother *I Am to Find My Ultimate Fulfillment in Motherhood* Mommy Guilt Is Just Something I Have to Live With *It's Wrong for Me to Go to God Again and Again After I Fail* Theology Isn't for Moms *I Have to Be a Perfect Mom* I Have to Do it All *I Am Enough* My Children Would Be Better Off Having a Different Mom *I'm a Bad Mom* I'm Selfish If I Have Any "Me Time" *I Need a Lot of "Me Time"* Motherhood Has to Be Hard (And Hard Is Bad!) *I Have to "Keep My Act Together"* I Can't Have a Clean House While Raising Children *My Life Is Passing Me By* *I Am Responsible for My Child's Happiness* I Can't Do This Whole "Mothering Thing" *My Success as a Mom Is Directly Tied to How My Children Turn Out* I Don't Know What It Means to Be a Mom If I Only Have One Child *I Don't Have Time* My Postpartum Body Has to Look a Certain Way *Children Are a Nuisance and an Interruption* Children Are Really Expensive *Children Ruin a Marriage* My Focus Should Be on Rules and Regulations *The "Experts" Know Better How to Raise and Educate My Child Than I Do* The Most Important Thing Is My Child's Education *Good Moms Do "XYZ"* You Have to "Do" Motherhood the Way the Culture Tells You

PART 2

Lies About How God Views Us as Moms

Motherhood Is a Woman's Highest Calling *Mothering Is Unimportant Work* My Identity Is to Be Found in Being a Mother *I Am to Find My Ultimate Fulfillment in Motherhood* Mommy Guilt Is Just Something I Have to Live With *It's Wrong for Me to Go to God Again and Again After I Fail* Theology Isn't for Moms *I Have to Be a Perfect Mom* I Have to Do it All *I Am Enough* My Children Would Be Better Off Having a Different Mom *I'm a Bad Mom* I'm Selfish If I Have Any "Me Time" *I Need a Lot of "Me Time"* Motherhood Has to Be Hard (And Hard Is Bad!) *I Have to "Keep My Act Together"* I Can't Have a Clean House While Raising Children *My Life Is Passing Me By* *I Am Responsible for My Child's Happiness* I Can't Do This Whole "Mothering Thing" *My Success as a Mom Is Directly Tied to How My Children Turn Out* I Don't Know What It Means to Be a Mom If I Only Have One Child *I Don't Have Time* My Postpartum Body Has to Look a Certain Way *Children Are a Nuisance and an Interruption* Children Are Really Expensive *Children Ruin a Marriage* My Focus Should Be on Rules and Regulations *The "Experts" Know Better How to Raise and Educate My Child Than I Do* The Most Important Thing Is My Child's Education *Good Moms Do "XYZ"* You Have to "Do" Motherhood the Way the Culture Tells You

LIE #5

Mommy Guilt Is Just Something I Have to Live With

Here is an area where the good news of the gospel really comes into play and is found to be oh-so-applicable for our day-to-day lives as moms!

If you're a mom (even if you have only been one for a matter of days) you have undoubtedly already felt it—that sinking feeling gnawing at the pit of your stomach which is the quintessential sign that you are experiencing mommy guilt.[14] We have all faced that struggle at one time or another (or a hundred times, if we were completely honest!). Is this what the Lord would have for us, though? Is it His desire that we would feel this pain in our hearts, this feeling that we are guilty of failure as moms? Is our only option to struggle through our lives with the pain and regret associated with mommy guilt, just trying our best to keep the guilt to a minimum?

No, dear mama, not at all! I do not believe for a moment that this is the Lord's heart towards His daughters or the only option with which we have been left. In fact, I see many problems with today's epidemic of mommy guilt.

Mommy Guilt Oftentimes Isn't Even Based on Biblical Standards

One of the biggest problems with mommy guilt is that, more often than not, the guilt we're feeling is not due to a failure on our part to live up to true Biblical standards. Instead, the most common cause of mommy guilt today is a situation wherein we believe we have failed to live up to what are really just a list of popular cultural standards of mothering. These are standards which are simply the subjective man-made expectations of another person—someone we have learned from on a blog or followed on social media, a neighbor, a family member, a lady at our church or in our Bible study group, or a friend. We feel as if we have failed as moms when we don't do things exactly the same way we perceive someone else to be doing them (whether that perception is even true or not). We see ourselves as failures and then begin to subsequently experience mommy guilt if we are not daily implementing some sensory playtime activity for our littles or if we are not hosting elaborate Pinterest-inspired birthday parties every year or if we are not providing our children with all-organic meals from morning 'til night.

While all of these endeavors are great, they are not found in the Scriptures. Our Lord has not said in His Word that we must do these things or else we are sinning as moms and scarring our children for life. With that realization in mind, we can let go of the guilt associated with not making homemade play dough for our children or not taking them to the park every single day or not making gourmet meals or not teaching our children how to read at age three. If our children truly desire that we do these things, then sure. If we are able, I think it's important to implement some of those special, fun activities with our kiddos—we do want to make their fleeting childhood a memorable, precious time. We simply need to keep in mind that on those days when we do not do those things, that's OK, too. It really is, mama! The Lord is far more concerned about the truly Biblical concepts of us praying with our children, teaching them about Christ, pointing them to Him, and showing them every day just how much we love and value them, than He is the playtime activities we are involved in together.

There is so much freedom when we understand that! Jesus said in Matthew 11:28-30, "Come to Me, all you who labor and are heavy laden, and I will give you rest. Take My yoke upon you and learn from Me, for I am gentle and lowly in heart, and you will find rest for your souls. For My yoke is easy and My burden is light." Shake off the burden of trying to live up to man-made standards, dear mama, and instead embrace the Lord and His freeing ways.

Guilt Does Not Come from the Lord

Another problem with mommy guilt is that, as Christians, we need to remember that it is Satan who brings guilt, not Christ. This is true even when it is guilt experienced as a result of having not lived up to a true Biblical standard (and not merely a man-made one). That guilt does not come from the Lord and is not something He wants us to carry around. If we have been saved, the following passages reveal how God now views us and what our true standing is before Him:

> There is therefore now no condemnation for those who are in Christ Jesus....what then shall we say to these things? If God is for us, who can be against us? He who did not spare his own Son but gave him up for us all, how will he not also with him graciously give us all

> things? Who shall bring any charge against God's elect? It is God who justifies. Who is to condemn?
>
> —Romans 8:1, 31-34a

> And every priest stands daily at his service, offering repeatedly the same sacrifices, which can never take away sins. But when Christ had offered for all time a single sacrifice for sins, he sat down at the right hand of God, waiting from that time until his enemies should be made a footstool for his feet. For by a single offering he has perfected for all time those who are being sanctified...... Let us draw near with a true heart in full assurance of faith, with our hearts sprinkled clean from an evil conscience and our bodies washed with pure water.
>
> —Hebrews 10:11-14, 22

> Therefore, since we have been justified by faith, we have peace with God through our Lord Jesus Christ.... Since, therefore, we have now been justified by his blood, much more shall we be saved by him from the wrath of God.
>
> —Romans 5:1, 9

You see, our Lord is not in the business of heaping guilt upon our shoulders. Ever. As His children, God does not view us as being guilty of wrongdoing. When He saved us, He forever took away all the guilt and shame our sins—past, present, and future—had produced, separating us from them as far as the east is from the west (Psalm 103:12) and forever removing our sin and guilt from His mind (Isaiah 43:25). At the moment of salvation, we put off the old man with its sin and shame (Colossians 3:9-10) and became new creations in Christ (2 Corinthians 5:17), perfect in God's eyes and now possess Christ's righteousness as our very own (Philippians 3:9, 2 Corinthians 5:21). When God looks at us, He sees Christ and His perfect holiness. That's it. It is as if we have never sinned—that is the true beautiful result of the doctrine of justification by faith. As Romans 5:9 shows, the full wrath of God which we deserved as a result of our sin was poured out on Christ instead, forever saving us from that wrath.

To believe, then, that our Lord is all right with us walking around in defeat, enveloped in mommy guilt every day of our lives, is to harbor a complete misunderstanding of the gospel, the substitutionary atonement of Christ, and the very heart and love of God Himself.

In Isaiah 53, Jesus is described as having "borne our griefs" and "carried our sorrows" (vs. 4), so that in Psalm 34:5, God's people can then accurately be described as "radiant" and unashamed. When we walk in defeat weighed down by mommy guilt, we are showing the true condition of our hearts. We may believe in our minds the truth of our new position in Christ, but down deep in our hearts we are not allowing that truth to affect our everyday lives. When the lies of the enemy invade and we are tempted to believe we are guilty, we end up listening to those lies rather than being faithful to take every thought captive, comparing them to God's truth. We are either believing Christ's atonement and our resulting justification to be insufficient, or else we believe them to solely affect our eternal destiny, but not the here and now everyday life we live. Either way, we are inadvertently rendering Christ and His atonement as lacking in power.

I don't know about you, but I no longer want to grieve the heart of God my Savior by buying into these lies of mommy guilt and condemnation.

Sweet sisters in Christ, hear me when I say that mommy guilt is not what the Lord has for you! One of my favorite books, *Pilgrim's Progress*, begins with the main character, Christian, being weighed down by a huge burden on his back of sin, guilt, shame, and condemnation. What is most noteworthy is the fact that when Christian finds salvation at the foot of the cross, that burden falls off. He doesn't trust in Christ and then continue to carry the burden with the only difference being that he now at least has a heavenly eternity to eagerly anticipate. No. That burden of sin and guilt completely falls off! It's forever gone. He is no longer under it. This is exactly the way it should be for us, mama.

In Romans 8:37, Paul describes the people of God as being "more than conquerors" through Christ our Savior. Lay hold of that characterization that is yours in Christ, claiming that truth for yourself day in, day out. Believe it with all your heart, mind, soul, and strength. Believe it down deep in your toes and have it make a difference in the way you live your life and view your motherhood. If you do, the result will be such an unwavering joy as you go throughout your days of mothering, that your living testimony will point the watching world to the Savior. Be ready—such a rare outlook on life as this will likely cause people to begin inquiring about the "hope that is in you" (1 Peter 3:15). What an opportunity!

The Difference Between Conviction and Condemnation

At this point, you may be wondering whether what you are feeling in the pit of your stomach on those hard days is just mommy guilt that you need to be freed from or true conviction from God (and how exactly you can know the difference!). The first thing would be to go back to what we talked about at the beginning and ask yourself if the issue you are feeling like a failure over is merely an expectation of man or a true command of God. If it is the first one, you can rest assured it is simply mommy guilt that you are heaping upon yourself, and you need to let go of it. If, however, the issue at hand in your mothering is a case of you not following an actual command from God, you have to assess exactly what is going on in your heart, asking yourself what that gut feeling is motivating you to do.

In a situation where you are experiencing sadness over actual sin in your mothering, is it a case of guilt and condemnation or an appropriate feeling of Holy Spirit conviction? The answer to this is found in whether that sadness is inspiring you to run towards God or away from Him. In the case of true conviction from God, we will feel a sense of sadness over our sin, but that sadness will not ultimately result in our wanting to hide ourselves from God in shame, despairing that we will never gain victory in this area of sin. It will not keep us from wanting to seek God's face and His help, nor will it tempt us into giving up on this whole sanctification thing. These feelings are not evidence of God convicting us, but of Satan condemning us.

It is true that the Holy Spirit is always working to teach, sanctify, and convict us. Do not confuse this, however, with Him condemning us or heaping guilt upon our heads—we have already seen that there is no condemnation for the people of God; He removed all our guilt when He died for us. There is a big difference between a conviction that you are doing something wrong and a condemnation or feeling of guilt. The first one will inspire you to change and fill you with hope that such change is possible through the help of the Holy Spirit of God. The second one will drive you to despair and hopelessness, believing yourself to be a hopeless case, forever unable to please Him.

Rather than it being the Lord who produces feelings of guilt in our hearts, it is Satan who does this to us. Revelation 12:10 says, "And I heard a loud voice in heaven, saying, 'Now the salvation and the power and the kingdom of our God and the authority of his Christ have come, for the accuser [i.e., Satan] of our brothers has been thrown down, who accuses them day and night before our God.'" Did you catch that? Satan is the accuser of the people of God. As such, he wants to beat us down, defeating us and making us think we are incapable of living lives to the glory of our Savior. Satan writhes in disgust and defeat when the people of God actually rise up and begin living lives which accurately represent their new position in Christ. He can't handle it, so he implements one of his biggest lies—a lie which is believed by all too many mamas: that God views us as guilty failures when we make mistakes.

I sit here in my recliner typing away this morning with a feeling of desperation in my soul, a deep-seated desire that you would finally, fully grasp down deep in your toes what your new position is in Christ. Please see it, mama! You are redeemed. You have been made new. In the eyes of God, you are not guilty. You are not condemned. You are not a disappointment or a failure. You are a new creation in Christ, everything about your old self has passed away, your sins (past, present, and future) have all been forgotten by God, your guilt was nailed to the cross, and when the Father looks at you, He sees Christ's perfection. He sees the law perfectly fulfilled. He sees garments of white. Do you see now why it is such a travesty and downright lie for us as moms to walk around believing that we are guilty and just have to live with feelings of mommy guilt? We do not have to live that way anymore, ladies! We can choose to take those thoughts of guilt captive and forever live in victory and peace before God our Father on a day-to-day basis.

Our enemy can't bear for us to fully understand our true position in Christ because, if we do, if we shake off the chains of guilt and shame in which Satan has endeavored to trap us, if we instead know the truth and allow the Gospel to fight off the lie that mommy guilt is unavoidable, we will live in freedom, victory, and holiness before God, all of which are a huge attack on Satan and his endeavors in this world.

Go Forth in Freedom, Mama!

I know first-hand how pervasive the feeling of mommy guilt can be. I've been there, and I know how much it hurts. And while it is true that we all have areas of our motherhood in which we do need to grow, the Lord desires to lovingly and gently come alongside us, helping to spur us forth in the ongoing sanctification of our mothering. He does not, however, desire to heap burdens of guilt upon us. Christ, through His sacrifice on the cross, has forever freed us from the bondage of guilt and shame. We need to embrace and believe this truth for ourselves, walk joyfully in it, and live out this freedom in front of our children—doing so is one of the most powerful ways in which we can illustrate for them the good news of the gospel in a tangible, everyday life sort of way.

So, go forth in freedom and grace today, dear mama! May these truths we've studied today set you free from the lies and bondage of mommy guilt, and may you be free indeed (John 8:32).

Motherhood Is a Woman's Highest Calling *Mothering Is Unimportant Work* My Identity Is to Be Found in Being a Mother *I Am to Find My Ultimate Fulfillment in Motherhood* Mommy Guilt Is Just Something I Have to Live With *It's Wrong for Me to Go to God Again and Again After I Fail* Theology Isn't for Moms *I Have to Be a Perfect Mom* I Have to Do it All *I Am Enough* My Children Would Be Better Off Having a Different Mom *I'm a Bad Mom* I'm Selfish If I Have Any "Me Time" *I Need a Lot of "Me Time"* Motherhood Has to Be Hard (And Hard Is Bad!) *I Have to "Keep My Act Together"* I Can't Have a Clean House While Raising Children *My Life Is Passing Me By* *I Am Responsible for My Child's Happiness* I Can't Do This Whole "Mothering Thing" *My Success as a Mom Is Directly Tied to How My Children Turn Out* I Don't Know What It Means to Be a Mom If I Only Have One Child *I Don't Have Time* My Postpartum Body Has to Look a Certain Way *Children Are a Nuisance and an Interruption* Children Are Really Expensive *Children Ruin a Marriage* My Focus Should Be on Rules and Regulations *The "Experts" Know Better How to Raise and Educate My Child Than I Do* The Most Important Thing Is My Child's Education *Good Moms Do "XYZ"* You Have to "Do" Motherhood the Way the Culture Tells You

LIE #6

It's Wrong for Me to Go to God Again and Again After I Fail

To piggy-back off the lie we just looked at in regards to mommy guilt, I want to address a corresponding issue that one of my blog readers, Lena, raised when she shared the following struggle she often deals with in her motherhood:

> [I believe] that I don't deserve God's blessing if I have been failing in being a good mother or with my Bible reading, etc. I feel unworthy to come and ask for grace and forgiveness again!! [Even though] I know as our Father He desires to keep giving us grace because He knows we will fail daily!

I so appreciated Lena sharing her heart like this because I find this to be another area many of us moms struggle with at one time or another. As we saw when addressing the issue of mommy guilt, only conviction comes from the Lord—not guilt or condemnation. Due to how Satan seeks to condemn us, however, it can be easy for us to feel so ashamed when we do not live up to God's standard in some way that the last thing we feel like doing is going to our Father, seeking His face in repentance, and asking for grace and forgiveness. We would rather just tuck our tail between our legs and go off and hide.

Here's where it gets interesting—did you catch the similarity between what we feel like doing when we sin and what Adam and Eve did in the Garden following their sin? They, too, hid from God. They didn't want to seek His face or be seen by Him, either. They didn't want to ask His forgiveness for their wrongdoing. While sin does naturally breed shame and feelings of guilt, I think this desire to hide rather than face the issue head-on and resolve it through repentance is a direct result of Satan lying to us again out of his desire to keep us out of close fellowship with God.

While Satan seeks to sow seeds of discord, disunity, and broken fellowship, our God pursues restoration, reconciliation, and intimacy with His people. This was Christ's very life purpose! He came that the vast canyon of sin and wrath between us and God might be bridged, resulting in a perfect unity with the Lord once more, just as it was in the Garden.

What the Lord Would Have Us Do

Our mission throughout this entire book is to train ourselves not to rely on our own hearts and minds, assuming our feelings and thoughts to be true, but to instead diligently take every single thought captive to the truth of God's Word. When we do, we will see our minds changed and renewed day by day. We also need to apply this practice to the lie we are addressing here and not ask ourselves what we feel like doing or feel worthy to do, but what our Lord would have us do when we sin and fall short again and again in our mothering. I believe there are five things He wants us to keep in mind during these times:

1. Grace and forgiveness are already ours.

Lena mentioned not wanting to ask the Lord for grace and forgiveness again and again. There is a sense in which we don't even have to. Do I believe that ongoing repentance is important in the life of the believer? Absolutely! I also believe, however, that the practice of repentance is more for us and the well-being of our own hearts, than it is for God, His approval, or His forgiveness. Repentance keeps us in daily reminder of God's standards for the way in which we are to live, the existence of our sin nature, and our ongoing need for Him. The practice of repentance keeps us in a right posture before God—one of humility and a desire for obedience and faithfulness to Him.

Following salvation, however, repentance is not something we do again and again in order to earn God's forgiveness or to receive His grace. If we think it is, then we have a false view of salvation or, at the very least, an incomplete understanding of it. As we addressed previously, at the moment of salvation every sin—past, present, and future—was forgiven, removed from us as far as the east is from the west, forgotten by God, and forever blotted out. In its place was imputed the righteousness of Christ, the grace of God, and a right standing before Him. From that moment on, we daily live under grace, not condemnation, as the children of God.

So, when it comes to repentance, we do not practice it out of a desire to receive God's grace and forgiveness—we already have them! Rather, repentance is the means by which we keep our hearts and minds in the right place before Him. Instead of stressing over the need to repeatedly ask God for grace and forgiveness, thank Him for His grace and forgiveness that are already yours—today and everyday—as a child of the King.

2. We need to have a right understanding of God.

How we approach these instances of sin in our lives depends on our view of God. This is why, in the next lie we address, we will delve into the big picture of why a right theology is so important for motherhood. The way we view God, what we believe about His character, and what we picture

His heart being towards us as His children will all color our day-to-day lives and how we live out our calling as moms.

When we sin again (as we always do—just ask Paul!), do we picture Him as being disappointed in us, disgusted with how we have fallen yet again, ashamed that He would ever have called us His own children and wishing that we would just shape up and finally get our act together once and for all? If that is what we believe about God, that viewpoint will influence our actions and lead to our cowering off in a corner somewhere, feeling incapable or unworthy of coming to Him when we fall.

If, however, we know that when God looks at us, He only sees Christ; if we believe what we studied in the previous chapter regarding our true standing before Him; and if we truly grasp the depth of His great love for us, then we will confidently come to Him when we sin, viewing Him as our loving Father. Yes, we will be grieved that we sinned against Him, and we know He will be grieved over our sin, as well—not because He is fed up with us or disdaining of the weakness of our flesh, but because this old sin nature is not what He intended for us, and it grieves His father heart to see His children stumbling, committing sins, and reaping the natural consequences thereof.

Here is something we all need to remember in these instances of repetitive sin: the Lord is not surprised by them. Not a bit. He already knows the old flesh is something we will continually have to do battle with this side of Heaven (Romans 7). To illustrate this, just think about what Christ said in Matthew 18. He was asked by His disciples if they had to forgive their brother again and again when he sinned against them, even up to seven times. Jesus' answer is amazing—He wanted them to keep on forgiving their sinning brother over and over again, up to "seventy times seven" (vs. 21 and 22). Evidently, Jesus fully expected people to still struggle with sin again and again on this side of glory. We need to stop assuming, then, that God is up in Heaven astounded that

His children are still struggling with sin issues, even as they are on the road of sanctification. If we would remember that our sinful tendencies do not catch Him by surprise, I think it would be a little easier for us to go to Him when we do fall.

3. He actually wants you to come to Him!

How do you feel, mama, when your children disobey you? Do you want them to cower in a corner somewhere, afraid to look at you, feeling too ashamed to come to you in repentance, and feeling unable to restore the close fellowship you enjoyed before the disobedience took place? No, of course not! You love your children so much that you want them to run to you, to admit that what they did was wrong, but to know that you are a safe place to which they can run—a place where they will always find the forgiveness and reconciliation they seek. As their mama, you want to throw your arms around them and shower them in love, right?

Now, take that feeling and understand that this is precisely how our Heavenly Father feels towards us, His children. Though you may feel the shame and weight of your sin, embarrassed to go to your Father, this is not how He wants you to feel. He wants you to know you are safe in His arms, loved with an everlasting love, and always welcome to come to Him, knowing that you will be received into His arms with great joy, much as the prodigal son was when he returned home and was greeted by his own father (Luke 15:11-32). You will not be beaten over the head with the reality of your sin, you will not be asked why on earth you have failed yet again, you will not cause God to wonder why you can't just get your act together, or why you expect Him to restore a right relationship yet again. He will just be so pleased that you did come to Him.

We must remember this: Satan is the one who wants us to go as far in the opposite direction of God as we can after we sin; God is the one who always wants us to draw near to Him after we fall that He might help us back up and set us back on the right path once more.

4. We aren't worthy or deserving—that's what makes it amazing grace!

Lena mentioned believing that she doesn't "deserve God's blessing if [she has] been failing in being a good mother or with [her] Bible reading, etc. [She feels] unworthy to come and ask for grace and forgiveness". To be quite honest, this particular portion of Lena's struggle is not actually founded on a lie. We simply do not deserve God's blessing—ever. Nothing good we do could ever make us deserving of His blessing, so a new sin we commit today does not suddenly render us undeserving of His goodness.

When Adam chose to shirk the authority of God in his life way back in the Garden of Eden and instead set out on his own path doing what was right in his own eyes (Judges 17:6, Proverbs 12:15), he instantly and for all time rendered all of us undeserving of God's blessing, grace, mercy, kindness, and forgiveness. But, praise be to God, the story did not end there! And that is precisely what is so amazing about grace. If we did deserve it, it would not be grace. Grace is "unmerited favor", and our loving God chose to bestow that blessing upon us—not as a result of our somehow deserving it, but out of the immense kindness and goodness of His heart.

5. His mercies are new every morning.

Lamentations 3:22-23 has to be one of the most comforting passages in all of Scripture:

> Through the Lord's mercies we are not consumed, Because His compassions fail not. They are new every morning; Great is Your faithfulness.

I especially love reading these verses in the context of being a mom. How often do we, as moms, feel like complete and utter failures? How often do we go to bed thinking, *I swore that today I would not yell at my kids and then I totally blew a gasket* or *I said I was going to be more intentional about getting down on the floor to play with my little ones, but I didn't do that once today*? Sound familiar at all? Just picture me raising my hand right now alongside you! We have all had those moments as moms. The beautiful truth of the gospel, though, is that we don't have to give in to those feelings. We don't have to harbor that despair in our hearts—not if we know the God of the Bible and the good news of His gospel!

We have been faithfully promised that His mercies and compassions are new every morning—every single morning we get a re-start. No matter what! It doesn't matter if you yelled at your kids yesterday or failed to give them the kind of dedicated time and attention you should have. God's mercies and compassions are still brand new for you this morning, on this new day you have to walk with the Lord. Let that truth sink down deep into your heart today and allow the overflow of that joy, love, and peace to carry out into your home, your marriage, and your interactions with your children. It will make all the difference in the world!

Motherhood Is a Woman's Highest Calling *Mothering Is Unimportant Work* My Identity Is to Be Found in Being a Mother *I Am to Find My Ultimate Fulfillment in Motherhood* Mommy Guilt Is Just Something I Have to Live With *It's Wrong for Me to Go to God Again and Again After I Fail* Theology Isn't for Moms *I Have to Be a Perfect Mom* I Have to Do it All *I Am Enough* My Children Would Be Better Off Having a Different Mom *I'm a Bad Mom* I'm Selfish If I Have Any "Me Time" *I Need a Lot of "Me Time"* Motherhood Has to Be Hard (And Hard Is Bad!) *I Have to "Keep My Act Together"* I Can't Have a Clean House While Raising Children *My Life Is Passing Me By* *I Am Responsible for My Child's Happiness* I Can't Do This Whole "Mothering Thing" *My Success as a Mom Is Directly Tied to How My Children Turn Out* I Don't Know What It Means to Be a Mom If I Only Have One Child *I Don't Have Time* My Postpartum Body Has to Look a Certain Way *Children Are a Nuisance and an Interruption* Children Are Really Expensive *Children Ruin a Marriage* My Focus Should Be on Rules and Regulations *The "Experts" Know Better How to Raise and Educate My Child Than I Do* The Most Important Thing Is My Child's Education *Good Moms Do "XYZ"* You Have to "Do" Motherhood the Way the Culture Tells You

LIE #7

Theology Isn't for Moms

If there is one thing that grieves my heart the most when it comes to the misconceptions surrounding motherhood that women are buying into today, it is the idea that the practice of studying theology is not for mom and that moms are just "too busy" to be in the Word of God on a regular basis. We will specifically address the time aspect of this lie when we get to lie #23, but right now I want us to focus on the aspect that says that studying theology simply is not worthwhile or applicable for moms.

To put it plainly, nothing could be further from the truth! This is perhaps the cleverest lie Satan plants into our minds because from it flows all the other lies with which we could ever struggle. Every lie that we believe as moms stems from a lack of knowledge of the truth. Otherwise, we would not fall prey to believing lies. Instead, we need to be just as the bank manager who knows from detailed study what a real dollar bill looks like, so that he is then able to spot a counterfeit one a mile away. It is my desire to see us as moms become just as well-versed in the Word of God that we are likewise able to sniff out a lie from a mile away. The only way we will ever get to that point, however, is if we first understand that theology is, in fact, for moms!

How Theology Benefits Our Motherhood

When we say we are too busy to be in the Word of God and therefore do not make studying theology a priority, what we are actually saying is that we believe God's Word is unimportant. Or, at the very least, that it is important as far as salvation goes, but then its relevant nature stops there. I want to dispel that myth for you once and for all, mama, and hopefully, in so doing, help instill in you such a deep hunger and love for God's Word (and understanding of your need for it!) that you can't help but get into it on a regular basis.

The Word is the Very Instruction Manual for our Mothering

It's always sad to see the memes shared on Facebook that speak to the wish parents have that babies would be born with an instruction manual. Here's the thing: if we are Christians, we know that they have been! It's the Word of God. Paul tells us in 2 Timothy 3:16-17 that "All Scripture is given by inspiration of God, and is profitable for doctrine, for reproof, for correction, for instruction in righteousness, that the man of God may be complete, thoroughly equipped for every good work." Complete and thoroughly equipped. That means that if we believe motherhood to be a good work (and we can rest assured that it is), then everything we need to be fruitful, productive, and capable in our mothering is found in the Word of God. This also means that the flip side is likewise true—without the Word of God, we are not equipped for our work as moms. That realization alone should drive us to open our Bibles, believing the theology found therein to be incredibly applicable and relevant to our mothering.

We Need Right Theology More Than We Need More Parenting Books

When facing some quandary of what to do in a particular area of our mothering, whether it is a baby's sleep issues, a toddler's temper problem, or a teen's behavioral challenges, our tendency as moms is to first jump to seek the input of the parenting "experts" online or to head to the bookstore to pick up the latest parenting book from a world-renown pediatrician. This is to be expected by moms who are not Christians and do not believe in God and the power of His Word. But why would we, as Christians, jump to seek the advice of someone who is an "expert" in the world's eyes when we have access to God Himself, the maker of Heaven and Earth, the very designer of our children and their personalities? We'll take the time to read the books and the blogs, but we won't take that same time to instead open up our Bibles and sit in communion with the Lord?

What we so often forget is that the Lord knows our own unique child; the pediatrician or "expert" does not. While the parenting books may offer some benefit, the methods they contain do not work for all children, for all children are so incredibly different having been specially hand-designed by God. So, while the parenting books work for some, God's Word works for all. In James 1:5, we are promised that "If any of you lacks wisdom, let him ask of God, who gives to all liberally and without reproach, and it will be given to him." Notice the wording there—it *will* be given (not might be or will be if you ask hard enough!). It will undoubtedly be given to you when you ask for it. Not only that, it will be given liberally. When you are in need of wisdom for what to do in a particular parenting situation, go to the Lord in faith, knowing He will liberally give you all the wisdom you could ever need for what you are going through. "The fear of the Lord is the beginning of wisdom, and the knowledge of the Holy One is understanding" (Proverbs 9:10).

It basically comes down to this question: do you believe this to really be true? Your view as to the importance of theology all depends on what your priorities are and whether or not you believe the Word of God to be as the writer of Hebrews claimed it is—alive, active, and powerful. Because, if you do, you'll run to it every chance you get, seeking the answers needed for your every parenting struggle.

Theology Provides Us with Hope When the Going Gets Tough

We already know that a right theology is crucial for raising our children well and for understanding what we are to do in any given situation. More than that, theology also girds us with hope when the going gets tough.

Theology is simply "the study of God", and Jesus, in John 17, spoke to the crucial importance of knowing God in order for us to be able to faithfully live in this world and not of it, equating knowing God with eternal life itself (vs 3). Jesus knew we would face trouble in this world (John 16:33), so in His prayer to the Father on our behalf in John 17, He asked that we would be kept close to Him, remembering what He had taught, and be united in His promises. Again, for all aspects of our motherhood, knowing the Word and, through it, knowing God Himself is what is most crucial.

Now, I want to speak for a moment to the importance Jesus placed on knowing God and point out that He was not saying this was only the case for men. Theology is not merely for men—it's just as much for women and moms, too, which is precisely why I included this lie in the section of the book dealing with how God views us. If we know God, truly understand His heart towards women and the worth and importance He gave to them, we would not be embracing this ridiculous lie that theology is not for moms. We would not, in essence, believe that God would have us live under the mistaken cultural idea of ancient Israel in which women were not to be taught the Word of God (which, in that day, was the Torah, the first 5 books of the Old Testament).

Perhaps without realizing it, when we say we are too busy to study the Word of God in this current season of mothering, what we are really saying is that the Word of God is not important or needed for the life we are living. We are essentially buying into the chauvinist idea that women and the Word of God need not mix. That's no different than the way radical feminists will tell you that you are wasting your college education if you are "just a mom", as if mothering requires no grey matter. Contrary to popular cultural opinion, mothering—if it's going to be done right—requires you to actually use your brain! The question is, with what are you filling your brain? Is it daytime TV, reality shows, celebrity news, social media stats, and romance novels? Or, is it the powerful, unchanging, alive, active Word of God that never returns void (Isaiah 55:11) and has been designed to equip you for your everyday life?

Jesus is the Example for Your Motherhood

We know that being a student of the Word is so necessary for mothering well. What I didn't realize until I heard Sally Clarkson say it, however, was just how applicable the life of Christ, specifically, is to our mothering. As Sally regularly points out, Jesus endured many of the exact same things we moms do on a daily basis; and therefore, he is the perfect example for how to endure hardship, sacrifice, unending work and ministry, exhaustion, and the never-ending needs of others with grace, love, selflessness, patience, and kindness. Jesus was well acquainted with having people clamor after Him day after day, oftentimes calling out to Him with their needs right when He was planning to set aside time to rest. He clearly understands what we go through as moms! He not only sees us in those hard moments of motherhood, but He has been there Himself. If you want to know how to be the kind of mom your kids need, the kind of mom you yearn to be, then look no further than the life and example of Christ. Everything you could possibly need in order to be equipped with wisdom, insight, love, grace, and truth for mothering can be found in Him. No other book on mothering can compare.

Get Reading, Mama!

I hope what we have discovered through addressing the lie that theology is not for moms has gotten you excited about the Word of God again. I encourage you to take even just a few minutes today to open up your Bible instead of Instagram, Netflix, or your favorite blog and just enjoy a bit of time soaking up the unchanging, never-ending, always-applicable wisdom of God. You will be comforted, refreshed, and invigorated as you do, and your mothering will change for the better!

PART 3

Lies About How We View Ourselves as Moms

Motherhood Is a Woman's Highest Calling *Mothering Is Unimportant Work* My Identity Is to Be Found in Being a Mother *I Am to Find My Ultimate Fulfillment in Motherhood* Mommy Guilt Is Just Something I Have to Live With *It's Wrong for Me to Go to God Again and Again After I Fail* Theology Isn't for Moms *I Have to Be a Perfect Mom* I Have to Do it All *I Am Enough* My Children Would Be Better Off Having a Different Mom *I'm a Bad Mom* I'm Selfish If I Have Any "Me Time" *I Need a Lot of "Me Time"* Motherhood Has to Be Hard (And Hard Is Bad!) *I Have to "Keep My Act Together"* I Can't Have a Clean House While Raising Children *My Life Is Passing Me By* *I Am Responsible for My Child's Happiness* I Can't Do This Whole "Mothering Thing" *My Success as a Mom Is Directly Tied to How My Children Turn Out* I Don't Know What It Means to Be a Mom If I Only Have One Child *I Don't Have Time* My Postpartum Body Has to Look a Certain Way *Children Are a Nuisance and an Interruption* Children Are Really Expensive *Children Ruin a Marriage* My Focus Should Be on Rules and Regulations *The "Experts" Know Better How to Raise and Educate My Child Than I Do* The Most Important Thing Is My Child's Education *Good Moms Do "XYZ"* You Have to "Do" Motherhood the Way the Culture Tells You

LIE #8

I Have to Be a Perfect Mom

We all want to be the very best moms we can possibly be for our children. We cherish the precious little lives God has entrusted into our care to raise. Therefore, the thought of letting them down or of doing a less-than-perfect job in mothering is heartbreaking to us. These feelings, though coming from a good place, can inadvertently lead to a lie with which so many of us moms struggle: the lie that we have to be perfect or else we will be ruining our children forever. Several ladies attested to their struggle when they shared the following comments with me on an Instagram post:

> I always feel the need to prove that I can do it all. Pull an income, keep everyone happy, keep the house, prepare regular healthy meals, keep up on laundry, and do it all to perfection. Wait, I still do struggle with this. But I forget about grace and being OK with less than perfect. I forget the people and focus too much on the things.
>
> —Caitlin

> [The lie I struggle with is] that we are supposed to be perfect. It's easy to forget that God gives us children for our own sanctification, as well.
>
> —Charity

> [I've believed] that anytime you make a parenting mistake you're ruining your child's life or scarring them forever.
>
> —Mary

How the Gospel Refutes This Lie

There are so many ways in which the good news of the gospel is able to aid us in combatting this lie of perfectionism. As with any lie we struggle with as moms, we are not left to our own devices in trying to get this lie out of our heads, fighting it in our own power with our own self-help mantras. Instead, we have the power of the Holy Spirit and the truth of God's Word to equip us in our pursuit of freedom from this idol of perfection.

There Is No Such Thing as the "Perfect Mom"

As we will discuss further when we get to lie #11, we first have to understand that there is no "perfect mom" floating around out there for us to tirelessly strive to emulate. The biggest problem with the lie that we have to be perfect is that, even though we know better, we are subconsciously believing in the facade that perfection is actually a possibility. In reality, the Word of God describes mankind's "good works" as being the equivalent of nothing more than filthy rags (Isaiah 64:6) and tells us that there is none righteous, no not one (Romans 3:10). To strive after the idol of perfection is to forget the gospel itself. After all, the gospel exposes our lingering imperfections. For if it were possible for us to become perfect on our own, we would have no need for Christ.

Perfectionism Distorts Our Child's View of the Gospel

Here's the thing: The Lord never asked you to be perfect for your kids. He merely asked you to point them to Him, being a conduit of the gospel through your imperfection. Our working towards perfection comes from a good place; after all, we want to be the best we can be for our children, to never let them down, and never hurt them. In all actuality, however, the greatest thing we could ever do for our little ones is point them to Jesus. What better way could we do that than by allowing them to see our own great need for Christ and His redemptive power that is alive and active within us? If our children never see their mommy stumble and fall flat on her face in sin, but then respond to such a fall by getting right back up, going to the Lord in repentance and faith, and then going on to live in the joy and peace which comes with knowing we're forgiven and have been made new, then how can we expect them to believe us when we say they need Jesus? If we are acting wise in our own eyes as if we have it all together and never struggle in any way, our children are never going to have an accurate representation of the depravity of man, the existence of the wrath of God towards sin, or our need for the great salvation that is offered to us through Christ.

Do your children a favor, mama, and stop trying to be perfect. Stop trying to make your kids think you have all the answers and point them instead to the One who does. Stop trying to "have it all together" and show them that you need Jesus, the One who puts all our broken pieces back together. Tell them about the sins and struggles you have dealt with all your life, but don't stop there. Tell them about the Lord who has redeemed you, share how He bought you with a price and made you His, and tell of how you were adopted into the family of God and made into a new creation in Christ. Tell them about the Helper you have in the Holy Spirit—the One who convicts you of sin, strengthens you when facing temptation, and encourages you when you experience the battles of spiritual warfare—and then make sure they know that the very same Helper is available to them. The fact of the matter is this: our children do not need perfect moms. They need moms who will point them to a perfect Savior.

Look to the Family Line of Christ

A bigamist and a liar, a prostitute and a man who lay with prostitutes, an adulterer and a murderer, a Moabite worshipper of foreign gods, one of the worst kings Israel ever had—these are the kinds of people God sovereignly chose to include in the family line of Jesus Christ (see Matthew 1:1-17). They were far from perfect, to say the least. Yet that didn't stop the Lord from using each one of them in powerful ways for the ultimate good of His Kingdom. In fact, I would say He used them specifically because of their great imperfections and sins. 1 Corinthians 1:26-31 says,

> For you see your calling, brethren, that not many wise according to the flesh, not many mighty, not many noble, are called. But God has chosen the foolish things of the world to put to shame the wise, and God has chosen the weak things of the world to put to shame the things which are mighty; and the base things of the world and the things which are despised God has chosen, and the

> things which are not, to bring to nothing the things that are, that no flesh should glory in His presence. But of Him you are in Christ Jesus, who became for us wisdom from God and righteousness and sanctification and redemption—that, as it is written, "He who glories, let him glory in the Lord."

Our Lord isn't interested in using the Pharisees of the world, the ones who can handle everything on their own, who think themselves to be perfect, and who view themselves as being in the possession of great self-righteousness. Rather, He uses the broken, sinful, debased people of the world. His glory is then able to be on full display when these very people are redeemed and made new in Him, going on to accomplish great things for His Kingdom through the strength He provides and His power which is made perfect in weakness.

When we remember this, who wants to be perfect anyway? It's not that we don't want to live lives of holiness, seeking to imitate Christ in all we say, think, and do. It isn't that we want to continue in sin that grace may abound (Romans 6:1-2). Of course not! It is true, however, that there is so much freedom, hope, and relief to be found in realizing that we simply do not have to be perfect; instead, the power of Christ rests upon us right in our weakness.

Remember That Christ Is in the Redemption Business

Mamas, we need to stop buying into our culture's lies of perfectionism. Instead, we need to exchange them for the truths of the gospel and start living like we actually believe in the redeeming power of God. We need to be living out the good news on a daily basis in front of our husbands, in front of our children, and in front of any neighbor, coworker, houseguest, or friend with whom we ever come into contact. Christian women these days have a terrible tendency to walk around in defeat and despair. This is completely inappropriate behavior for a daughter of the King of Kings. What reason do we have to despair? Why do we feel defeated? In case we have forgotten, God describes us in Romans 8:37 as being "more than conquerors" through Him. The same Holy Spirit power that raised Christ from the dead is living and active within us, as well. We have never-ending hope, peace, strength, love, and redemption power offered to us in Christ. And yet we fall into despair and feelings of mommy guilt when we fail to be "perfect". Let's refuse to buy into Satan's lies any longer, ladies. We are new creatures in Christ. Who then needs the world's standards of perfection or the never-ending tireless pursuit of that perfection? We have all we need in the One whose righteousness was imputed to our account at the moment of salvation. How's that for perfection!

The next time you are tempted to give into despair over your lack of perfection or the occurrence of yet another moment of sin in your life, stop looking to yourself and look up. Take your eyes off your sin and place them squarely on the Savior and Redeemer. Glory in the fact that He is in the business of redeeming everything: the years the locusts have eaten, your sinful tendency to yell at your children, your habit of expecting perfection from them, or whatever else is making you feel guilty. He can redeem all of it. But you have to believe that to be the case and live out that belief in front of your children. In doing so, you will be freeing yourself from the never-ending rat race of perfectionism and will instead be focusing your gaze on the only Perfect One, dancing in the freedom His grace has afforded you.

LIE #9

I Have to Do It All

Perhaps you can relate to the struggles of the following mamas:

> I always feel the need to prove that I can do it all. Pull an income, keep everyone happy, keep the house, prepare regular healthy meals, keep up on laundry, and do it all to perfection.
>
> —Caitlin

> I still feel there's a lot of pressure for moms to do it all well—clean house, crafts with kids, play dates, all while juggling your own hobbies (and for some, work outside the home too); it's a lot of pressure.
>
> —Hilary

> [I've believed the lie] that you can do it all.
>
> —Michelle

> [I struggle with believing] that we are supposed to be able to do it all! As a working mama, I'm exhausted. Emotionally, spiritually and physically. My house is a mess, I honestly hate the pressure of having 'company', and I don't find cooking for the family to be rewarding or satisfying in any way. I feel like I should be good at all of these things. I have no idea where this myth came from.
>
> —Aileen

Whether it stems from feminism's "you can have it all" mantra, our own man-made expectations, or even a misguided understanding of woman's God-given role of guardian of the home, we have somehow come to the conclusion that everything pertaining to home and family life depends on us. We believe ourselves to be the ones responsible for keeping the home spotless, making all the food for the family, running all the errands, hosting all the parties, chauffeuring our children to all the extracurricular activities, attending all the meetings, implementing all the discipline, and, to top it all off, earning an income to supplement the family economy. The superwoman myth then continues to rage, and women continue to be the losers.

The fact of the matter is this: when we believe everything depends on us and that we have to live up to all the expectations to which our culture calls us, we will always end up feeling as Aileen has—exhausted emotionally, spiritually, and physically. We will have no desire (or energy left over!) to look after the home front, practice hospitality, provide for our children's physical needs, or any of the other things we actually have been called by God to do.

Historically and culturally, this superwoman myth we are living under today largely stems from the feminist movement and its message that women can "have it all". However, what was once "women can have it all" or "women can do it all" (which are lies in and of themselves) has now become "women *should* do it all". Though this concept was propagated through the feminist movement, the idea actually found its ultimate conception in the mind of the enemy himself, who always seeks to take our eyes off what God has actually called us to and place them instead on what we think others expect of us. As we have already seen time and time again, Satan is the one who heaps burdens of guilt and "must-dos" upon our shoulders, stealing, killing, and destroying our lives (John 10:10a) in the process. Meanwhile, the Lord tells us that His yoke is easy and His burden is light (Matthew 11:28-30), and that He came that we might have abundant life (John 10:10b).

Ladies, we need to come to the realization that we were never made to be omnipresent or omnipotent and be content with that, leaving those abilities to the Lord. We cannot do it all. We can try, but at the end of the day, we will come up short if we try to fill shoes that we were never designed to wear. Something will always fall through the cracks when we add to our plates that which the Lord never intended for us to pursue.

On that note, I think we need to spend a minute discovering the truths found in Philippians 4:13, freeing this verse from the misconceptions that have been placed upon it by some in our day. Philippians 4:13 is in the Bible, and Paul does indeed say that we can "do all things through Christ who strengthens [us]". There are, however, two particular misconceptions we need to point out about this verse.

First, we need to be sure to look at it in its proper context. Paul is specifically speaking here in regards to his ability to—through the strength Christ gives—exercise contentment in the face of hardship and trial. It is more about how we can live in the midst of physical and emotional difficulty than it is about us performing certain tasks.

Second, while this verse teaches that we can do all things through the strength of Christ, the fact of the matter is we will be given strength for what God has called us to, not for what He hasn't. We are not free to run ahead of God and His will for our lives, adding this, that, and the other thing to our plates (things to which He has not called us), and then expecting the strength and stamina required to do it all. That's not how it works. Philippians 4:13 isn't saying we will be given strength so that we can do all the things we want to do. No, we will be given strength to endure all the things He Himself has called us to in each season of life. There's a big difference there. God is not our genie in a bottle at our beck and call to give us the strength required to do just anything we will to do. It's as my friend Naomi so wisely said during a podcast interview we recorded: "We as women are praying the wrong prayer. We are too busy asking God to help us juggle all the balls we have in the air when, in reality, we should be praying for wisdom to discern if there are any balls we're juggling that we need to lay down. We need to discern if we are juggling balls God never asked us to juggle in the first place."[15]

Anytime we try to take on one of the attributes of God which humans were never meant to possess, bad things happen. This first occurred in the Garden of Eden when Eve was promised by the serpent that she would become like God if she ate of the forbidden fruit. She liked the sound of that, and it was this desire to be like God that ruined everything. The same goes for us today. When we run ourselves ragged trying to be all things to all people and attempting to take on the omnipotent and omnipresent characteristics which belong to God alone, the end result is not good. We become worn out, burdened in ways the Lord never intended for us to have to endure.

The wording of Isaiah 30:15 is a beautiful reminder in this area: "In returning and rest you shall be saved; In quietness and confidence shall be your strength." Paul implemented the same concept when he wrote that we should "aspire to lead a quiet life" (1 Thessalonians 4:11) and "lead a quiet and peaceable life with all godliness and reverence" (1 Timothy 2:2). Our Lord values our living lives of peace, quiet, slowness, and rest. You can guess then what Satan values. He values our buying into the lie that we have to do it all. He values getting us moms worked up into a tizzy, believing the lie that we can't sit down and rest with our families because "there's work to be done." He values our being so preoccupied with our to-do list that we focus more on it than we do on our husbands, children, neighbors, and friends (you know, the truly important parts of life!). Satan wants us to possess a God-complex, thinking ourselves and our work to be indispensable, so that he can keep us distracted from spending time with God, playing with our children and teaching them Bible stories, sitting and chatting with our husbands, talking to the neighbor at the mailbox, or ministering in the community. Our marriages, families, and ministries are truly what are at stake when we buy into this clever lie from Satan that moms have to "do it all".

If Satan can get us to misplace our priorities, overwhelm our plates with things to do, and fill our schedules to the max, he can successfully keep us busy doing things which are of little eternal value while the truly important tasks are left undone. The result is that we end up disdaining those very tasks God has actually called us to perform, such as caring for our husbands and children and tending to our homes. When those tasks we thought we had to do wear us out and steal all our energy, we then become embittered against the tasks to which God *has* called us.

Women have a hard time believing Jesus when He says His yoke is easy and His burden is light (Matthew 11:28-30) because of the feelings of overwhelm and exhaustion they feel on a daily basis. Instead of listening to the voices inside our heads that try to tell us what we need to spend our time doing and then getting mad at God and doubting His goodness when we have no time or energy left for those things to which He called us, we need to begin every day first seeking His face. Let the lies of Satan, the culture, and your own head go, and instead seek God's will for your day. We are always saying we wish there were more than twenty-four hours in a day, but here's the deal—it is not by accident that God fashioned our days into periods of twenty-four hours. He has given us ample time for the tasks He has actually given us. Our problem (as we will see when addressing lie #23) is not that we don't have enough time. Our problem is that we are filling our time with the wrong things—things God never meant for us to pursue.

In many ways, it all comes down to a problem of fear. We fear that if we don't do "xyz", then the world will come to an end. We somehow believe the lie that if we don't finish all the laundry today, if we don't clean the whole house today, if we let the dishes sit in the sink tonight, if we don't run errands today, or if we don't teach our children multiplication today, then all will be lost. This is simply not true. We are not that powerful, mamas. Are those tasks important? Of course—we've already seen that to be the case. But they are not crucial. Meaning, if it doesn't all get done today, the world will not end and our children will not suffer. It may be cliché, but it's true—we need to let go and let God. At some point, we have to come to terms with trusting God and believing that He will make up for any shortcomings with which our day may have been filled. We have to believe Him when He says we are to "be still and know that [He is] God" (Psalm 46:10). The truth of the gospel is that we need to stop placing so much importance on what we accomplish and set our minds on what He has already accomplished for us.

A Word to the Proverbs 31 Woman

Some of you may be protesting right now because you think you see, in Proverbs 31, a picture of a woman who "did it all". Some of you may think it almost godly what you are doing with your thousand and one balls you're juggling because of all the ones we see the Proverbs 31 woman juggling. But here's the difference—she still had her priorities straight and kept first things first. Can we say the same of ourselves? When we attempt to "do it all", what suffers first? Our homes and our families do—neither of which is found to be suffering in Proverbs 31.

In the midst of everything, it is clear that the Proverbs 31 woman first "does [her husband] good and not evil all the days of her life" (vs. 12) and "watches over the ways of her household" (vs. 27a). We are responsible to make the most of the time God has given to us, being careful to redeem it well (Ephesians 5:16, Colossians 4:5). Part of redeeming time wisely, however, is not merely packing it with activity and work, but redeeming it specifically as God would have you redeem it: by keeping proper priorities in place, taking time to rest as He did, and so on. In order to faithfully redeem the time that has been given to us by God, we have to be using our time in a God-honoring way—not in a manner that gives way to Satan and his lies.

A Word to the Woman with No Help

Much of the time we get up in arms when we are told we don't have to do it all because we think if we don't do it, it won't get done. Perhaps your children are all too little to be of much help to you yet, and you have a husband who doesn't help much around the house. Guess what? You can ask for help! I know that goes against our pride, but sometimes our pride needs to be checked at the door. Most husbands are more than willing to help out around the house if they are asked. But you do need to ask. You can't expect your husband to read your mind or automatically know what needs to be done. Remember: the home is primarily your domain, and, as such, you know precisely how you like things to be, how you want tasks to be done, where you want things to go, etc. Why, then, are we surprised when our husbands don't just jump to the task at hand, dive in head first, and get it done? Many times, our husbands are probably just afraid they would do something wrong or perhaps they don't even know where to start. So, give your man some grace, extend to him the benefit of the doubt, and ask for his help.

Another thing I encourage wives to do is ask their husbands what household tasks mean the most to them. Which tasks would your husband prefer to find completed when he gets home from work? Would he love to find a home-cooked meal ready and waiting? Would he like to see the living room picked up? Would he prefer that the sink be empty of dishes? Ask your own unique husband what the most important couple of household chores are to him and focus your time on those first. Then, if those tasks are all you get done in a day, it will still have been a productive day—you will have put your husband first, shown him love through honoring his preferences, and you will have cut down on a lot of unnecessary stress that comes from thinking you have to "do it all". Be sure you actually ask, however, and don't just assume you know your husband's preferences! I was convinced I knew what my husband, Owen's, answer to this question would be, but ended up with quite a surprise!

If you are a woman reading this who does not have a helpful or supporting husband, please don't despair. Ask the Lord, your ultimate source of help (Psalm 121:2). He will give you wisdom to discern what needs to be done and what truly doesn't, how to go about performing the tasks that are most important, and help to see who in your circle of family and friends are the ones you could reach out to for assistance.

Jesus Didn't "Do it All"

As we will delve into deeper when addressing lie #13, we need to let go of our mistaken "Savior complex" of thinking we have to be all things to all people by realizing that Jesus Himself, the Savior of the world, didn't even "do it all". He didn't heal every infirmity, meet every need, or spend time with every crowd. In fact, there were many times when He sent crowds away and instead went off by Himself to pray and commune with the Father (for example, see Matthew 14:13-23). If even the Lord did not try to "do it all", why are we believing the lie that we are supposed to?

What Will You Choose Today?

So, what will it be, mama? Will you strive in vain again today to "do it all", or will you live your life at a more peaceful, restful pace doing all that the Lord has actually called you to and not what He hasn't? On that note, I want to leave you with the words Jesus said to Martha, a woman so very much like many of us. Don't bristle at His words. Instead, believe them to be coming from an all-wise, all-loving Savior, and embrace them as a help to your soul:

> Now it happened as they went that He entered a certain village; and a certain woman named Martha welcomed Him into her house. And she had a sister called Mary, who also sat at Jesus' feet and heard His word. But Martha was distracted with much serving, and she approached Him and said, "Lord, do You not care that my sister has left me to serve alone? Therefore tell her to help me." And Jesus answered and said to her, "Martha, Martha, you are worried and troubled about many

things. But one thing is needed, and Mary has chosen that good part, which will not be taken away from her.

—Luke 10:38-42

LIE #10

I Am Enough

I was scrolling through Facebook one day several months ago when I came across a post that had been shared upwards of a couple thousand times. Essentially, it was a short essay meant to be an encouraging open-letter to moms everywhere. The post started out great, addressing our problematic tendency to fall into mommy guilt, explaining that we are, in fact, doing a good job as moms, and so on. The problem came at the very end of what was otherwise a comforting essay, when the writer closed the post with these words: "Mom, you are enough."

I cringed reading that and found the beauty of the entire rest of the post to be adversely affected by the lie found at the end of it. I'm not at all trying to say that the author of the post was not coming from a good place or from what was assuredly a sincere and caring heart that simply desired to be an encouragement. I have no doubt this was the case. However, what was said at the end was, nevertheless, false. In fact, the real problem here is that, ironically, far from merely being false, this common sentiment is actually a hindrance to moms in their mothering.

When ladies shared with me on social media the most common lies they have been believing, Lisa said hers was:

> That I need to be enough.

It was such a breath of fresh air to read this comment because Lisa recognized it as a lie! It is disconcerting the development taking place today, where even Christian women are now believing that they—in and of themselves—are "enough". This humanistic philosophy is to be expected out in the world, but it has no place in the church. The problem is that we have taken the gospel of Christ and have begun to view it as solely affecting our eternity and the life to come, but being good for little in this life we are living in the here and now.

If we are going to begin believing the important truth that the gospel is not only for eternity, but also highly applicable to the here and now of our daily lives, then we are going to have to start applying its truths to the regular, everyday issues which arise in motherhood, not the least of which being this pervading cultural concept that "moms are enough". This lie stems from the idea that we can do this mothering thing on our own, when the fact of the matter is, we simply cannot.

Why You Won't Hear Me Say, "Mama, You Are Enough!"

For several reasons, I do not feel comfortable ever telling a fellow mama that she is enough. There are far more truly Biblical things I could be saying to her instead.

"I Am Enough" Deprives Moms of Their True Source of Strength

In those mothering moments when we are overwhelmed, stressed out, and feeling weak, the last thing we need is to be told we're enough. What we need is to be pointed in the direction of the lifeline. We need knowledge of, and access to, the only source of lasting strength (Philippians 4:13), our only hope and help (Psalm 121), and that is Christ. In 2 Corinthians 12:9-10, Paul writes, "And He said to me, 'My grace is sufficient for you, for My strength is made perfect in weakness.' Therefore most gladly I will rather boast in my infirmities, that the power of Christ may rest upon me. Therefore I take pleasure in infirmities, in reproaches, in needs, in persecutions, in distresses, for Christ's sake. For when I am weak, then I am strong."

Did you catch that? Realizing that on our own we are weak is not something to disdain or to mask with the band-aid of "I am enough." Instead, it is something to glory in and take pleasure from! For it is precisely when we are weak—not when we are feeling as if we have it all together, not when we are telling ourselves we are enough, but when we are weak—that the power of Christ rests upon us. I don't know about you, but I'm content with feeling weak if it means that in those moments the power of Christ will rest on me! I don't want to deprive myself of the strength which could otherwise be mine by believing the empty mantra that "I am enough"—a mantra which offers momentary comfort, perhaps, but no lasting benefit or help. Embrace your weakness in motherhood, mama. Don't shirk away from it, try to deny it, or disdain it. Instead, embrace it! For it is when you are weak that God will make you strong through Him. Nothing could be more beneficial on your hard days than knowing that!

"I Am Enough" Flies in the Face of the Gospel

The "Mama, you are enough!" concept is simply not true in light of the gospel, making it all the more unfortunate when Christian women buy into it. The fact of the matter is that if we, on our own, were enough, there would have been no reason for Christ to come and die on our behalf. Clearly, then, we are not enough, our deeds are not sufficient, and we are not all-powerful. This is why it is so important to take every thought captive. When we fail to do so, we inadvertently buy into the seemingly pleasant ideas of the culture, forgetting the truth of God's Word. We end up exchanging the strength of God that could be ours for the only thing the world can offer: the pitiful substitution of human strength.

"I Am Enough" Tells the Watching World That We Have Nothing Special to Offer

If we as Christian women are making the mistake of saying we are enough on our own, we are telling the world around us that the good news of the gospel really isn't so good after all. What we are essentially saying is that we don't have anything to offer them. If, as Christians, we are seen to be relying on our own strength, puffing ourselves up with the idea that we are enough, then we aren't going to look any differently than the world. We are not going to be putting the majesty, glory, strength, and power of God on full display. Instead, we will be making Christians look like fools. Imagine how it would look to you if you were not a follower of Christ and had a Christian first say to you that you are a lost sinner in need of Christ, but then later you heard that same Christian say, "I am enough". What would you think? Most likely you would believe that double-minded Christian not to be quite right in the head and assume that your supposed need for God must not be that big of a need after all.

There is great power in the words we say (Proverbs 18:21, James 3:5-6). What we think and say oftentimes leads to how we live. Make no mistake—in the case of this lie, living out of the belief that we are enough will affect our relationship with God and potentially inhibit our growth in Him. At the same time, it will render our Christian witness ineffective and faulty. We, as the body of Christ, have to begin to understand the seriousness of the words we say and the ramifications they have. Just as we are to take every thought captive to the obedience of Christ, we have to begin doing the same thing with our words as well, particularly when it comes to using common buzzwords from the culture. Everything we think and say needs to be compared to God's Word to see if it be true.

"I Am Enough" Tells Our Kids That Mommy Doesn't Need Jesus

This yields the same result as the one we just looked at regarding how our words affect the watching world's view of God, but it really hits home when we're talking about our own children and their view of Him. As we already saw, it's a good thing that we aren't perfect moms because we are able to tangibly embody for our children the vast need we all have for Christ and His work on the cross. The same goes for the lie that we have to "be enough" as moms. Not only do I know that I am not enough as a mom, I don't want to be! I don't want to steal the spotlight from my Lord. I don't want to fill a position only He was meant to fill and, in so doing, inadvertently tell my children that we don't need God and can be enough on our own. The souls of our children are at stake here. We need to reject the feeling of pride and self-sufficiency we receive when we believe we are enough. Instead, we need to rejoice in the truth that we simply are not enough on our own, but know Who is.

A Great Witnessing Opportunity

The next time people say to you, "Mama, you are enough!" kindly deny it. This may feel so counterintuitive, and you may be afraid that you'll come across as being down on yourself. However, if you thank them for their gracious desire to encourage you, but then point them to the truth of God's Word, just imagine what the impact could be! It could inspire them to begin totally rethinking their entire worldview and serve to point them to the power of God.

When it comes to encouraging fellow moms, let's no longer allow Satan's lies to get a word in edgewise. Satan wants us to feel self-sufficient and powerful in our own right, with no need for God and no desire to lean on Him. After all, he knows that if he can make this happen, he will be successful in weakening us and rendering both us and our witness powerless—even as we are thinking ourselves to be so strong. The truth is this: we don't want to encourage a fellow mama to be thinking she's enough. We want to be pointing her to the God Who is.

LIE #11

My Children Would Be Better Off Having a Different Mom

I'll never forget the night my son, James, was about two or three months old, and I was up at 3 a.m. crying in the bathroom over what a completely terrible mom I was. Following an overall super-easy experience with our firstborn (Anna was a fantastic sleeper from the very beginning, had to sometimes even be woken up for feedings as a newborn, and started sleeping through the night at two months old), came James.

He was completely different almost from day one. In the beginning, he was unwilling to sleep longer than forty-five minutes to one hour stretches at night unless he was being held, he was incredibly gassy (and therefore fussy) starting when he was one week old, and he was a night owl who didn't believe in going to sleep at a decent hour. There would sometimes be nights when, for whatever reason, he would wake up, nurse, and then not go back to sleep for an hour or more, fitfully alternating between crying and simply being wide awake. Such was the kind of night which found me crying my eyes out in the bathroom, gut-wrenchingly sure that my son would be so much better off if he had only been born to a mom with more patience, love, selflessness, and endurance than I possessed. Because let me tell you—on those incredibly difficult nights I, for the first time, really came face to face with the startling depths of my selfishness, discovering just how angry I can become when I'm sleep-deprived and don't get my way.

I'll never forget holding my baby boy that night, trying so desperately to get him to calm down and go to sleep so that I could go back to sleep myself, and feeling an overwhelming dark sense of rage and indignation welling up within me at the difficulty through which he was putting me. In that moment when I just wanted to scream, came the thoughts that were really all lies directly from Satan, though I didn't recognize them as such in that moment: *He would be better off without you. James should have been born to another mom. Other moms are far more patient, loving, warm, and selfless than you are. What's wrong with you? How could you be so angry at such an innocent little newborn baby?*

I felt like such a failure and, to be quite honest, a monster. How could I be mad at my baby? Why did God give James to such a raging, crazy woman? Then came the heartbreaking thoughts: *But I love my baby so much! I can't imagine him being born to someone else. I want him as mine, and yet I feel that being mine is such a disservice to him.* It's sobering just how easily Satan can get to you in the wee hours of the morning when you are a sleep-deprived mama! This is why it is so important to be on guard and ready with the Word of God. Because had I been, it would have been easier to take those dark and depressing thoughts captive—even in my exhausted state.

You see, the good news of the gospel and the truth of God's Word are applicable even to these lies, sweet mama! So, if you have ever felt, as I have, that your children were given to the wrong mom and would have been better off with someone else, I want you to remember the truth of God's Word and use it to combat those lies!

How God's Word Refutes This Lie

When we have been in the Word of God and know what it says, having allowed it to transform us by the renewing of our minds (Romans 12:2), it becomes easy to stop a lying thought such as this one dead in its tracks and intentionally counterattack it with the truth of the Bible. As it turns out, as with everything else we ever deal with in life, God has a lot to say about this sometimes-pervasive lie that our children would be better with a different mom.

Our God Is a Sovereign God

When I was crying in my bathroom that night, convinced that James would be better off being cared for by someone else, I was essentially saying that God had made a mistake. If I believe that my child should have had a different mom, then the fact of the matter is I am either believing God to not be all-powerful and sovereign, or I am thinking that He is in control, but was just guilty of making a mistake—neither of which could possibly be true.

In our American culture which worships at the altar of comfort and ease, we have bought into the mistaken idea that if something turns out to be hard or challenging, there must have been a mistake made somewhere. We must be doing the wrong thing, have the wrong assignment from God, or be dealing with the wrong set of circumstances since "hard equals bad", right?

What I needed to understand in the bathroom that night was that just because I was facing a challenging situation in weakness (and, yes, with a sinful attitude towards my baby), did not mean I was the wrong mom for my child or that God had made a mistake. I needed to take those thoughts captive, remembering the many accounts in God's Word of God's people going through hard and trying times, sinning and falling so far short of God's ways, and yet all still working out according to God's good, acceptable, and perfect will (Romans 12:2b) as a part of His ultimate plan (Isaiah 46:10).

A perfect example of this is found in the context of what has become an incredibly popular verse from Jeremiah 29: "For I know the thoughts that I think toward you, says the Lord, thoughts of peace and not of evil, to give you a future and a hope." (vs. 11). While we have the tendency to take this verse and run with it, imagining it to be promising us days of ease, comfort, and unending happiness, what is really being promised is the encouraging truth that in spite of the hardship, trial, difficulty, and heartache that we will surely face in this sin-cursed world, God's plans are still ultimately in motion. He is still working everything together for our good (Romans 8:28), and we can rest in Him no matter what is going on around us.

How do we know? Because we find that when we read this verse in its proper context, it was a reminder issued by God to His people, Israel, when they were in captivity in Babylon—not when they were out chilling on a beach somewhere enjoying a cold glass of iced tea. No, God offered this encouraging reminder when they were in captivity in a foreign land. If they could trust (at such a time) that God had not made a mistake, but rather believe He still had their best interests at heart in His perfect plan, then so can we when we're feeling as if God made a mistake regarding the mother of our children! We serve a sovereign God who knew our children when He was still forming them within us (Psalm 139:13-18), and He does not make mistakes. We can rest in that when the going gets tough.

You Are the Perfect Mom for Your Children

This truth flows from what we just saw regarding the sovereignty of God, but it bears repeating: you are the specific mom God chose for your children. That's a fact, plain and simple. Psalm 139 says that the Lord ordained all the days of our children's lives before even one came to be, and that He was the One who knit them together within us. Clearly, then, God intended for you to be your child's mom. So, if you, as my friend Angela has, ever find yourself struggling with the lie that "God didn't make me enough for my children", then you can strongly reject that sentiment knowing that you are the perfect one for the job God has chosen to give you.

We just finished looking at the lie "I am enough" as it regards our mistaken idea that we can do this mothering thing on our own and that, in and of ourselves, we are sufficient. There is, however, truth to the idea that we are enough for our children in that we are exactly the mom God designed for them just as we are. You, as your unique self, in the midst of your own sin patterns, strengths, and weaknesses, are enough for your children in the sense that God made you to be who you are, with your particular personality, gifts, and characteristics. Knowing this, we can rest in the fact that God knew what He was doing when He gave our children specifically to us to raise. Whether we feel like it is true or not, we are the moms the Lord wanted for our children.

The Lord Can Redeem Anything

This is where the good news of the gospel again proves itself to be so applicable to daily living. If we know the truth of God's Word and what it says about the Lord's great redemptive power, then we can rest in the fact that far from our children somehow being "better off" if they had a different mom, God is in the business of redemption and is quite good at what He does. No matter how we may fail, disappoint our children, or find our sin nature to be all-too-often on full display for them to witness, Joel 2:25 reminds us that the Lord can redeem and "restore to you the years that the locusts have eaten". No matter how our selfish tendencies or harsh and angry attitudes may arise in motherhood, they are never so powerful that the Lord cannot redeem them.

"There is None Righteous"

The lie that "my children would be better off having a different mom" stems from the myth that all other moms are perfect, and we are the only ones who struggle with various sins and imperfections. Sammie shared with me on social media that she has struggled with this lie herself:

> [I've believed] that everyone else's house is clean. That every mom cooks every night. That every mom is patient with her own kids and doesn't lose her cool as often as I do.

This is precisely what our old enemy, Satan, would have us think. If he can get us to believe this to be true, he can weaken our faith and dependence on God and encourage us to give in to despair. If he can get us to believe the lie that there's no hope for our old sinful selves, he can then make us feel incapable of intentionally training up our children in the way that they should go—with purpose, vision, strength, and joy.

So, reject the lie, mama. The future is at stake! Remember that the truth of the matter is that we are all on an equal playing field, having all sinned and fallen short of the glory of God (Romans 3:23). There is "none righteous" (Romans 3:9-12). I love how my friend, Jenn, put it: "[The lie I have believed] is that perfect moms exist."

If we see a fellow Christian mom who we think would be better for our children, then we need to remember in that moment that anything good we see in her is nothing of herself, but is a direct result of the Holy Spirit working within her. As redeemed sinners and children of God, we have access to that exact same power within us. As women who are now viewed by God to be saints, we need to stop this *woe is me, I'm such a sinner* mentality and start acting like the new creatures in Christ that we are, harnessing the power of the Holy Spirit within us. Romans 8:11 says, "But if the Spirit of Him who raised Jesus from the dead dwells in you, He who raised Christ from the dead will also give life to your mortal bodies through His Spirit who dwells in you."

Did you catch that? It was the Holy Spirit of God who raised Jesus from the dead, and that exact same power now resides within you. It's not that you are now made powerful in and of yourself (refer back to the lie about being enough), but that you now have access to the strength and power of God (2 Corinthians 12:9). He will redeem each sin and struggle in your life and sanctify you more and more into the image of Christ. The next time you feel yourself falling into that defeatist *I'll-never-be-good-enough, my-children-need-a-different-mom* mentality, stop believing Satan and start believing the Bible.

Motherhood Is a Woman's Highest Calling *Mothering Is Unimportant Work* My Identity Is to Be Found in Being a Mother *I Am to Find My Ultimate Fulfillment in Motherhood* Mommy Guilt Is Just Something I Have to Live With *It's Wrong for Me to Go to God Again and Again After I Fail* Theology Isn't for Moms *I Have to Be a Perfect Mom* I Have to Do it All *I Am Enough* My Children Would Be Better Off Having a Different Mom *I'm a Bad Mom* I'm Selfish If I Have Any "Me Time" *I Need a Lot of "Me Time"* Motherhood Has to Be Hard (And Hard Is Bad!) *I Have to "Keep My Act Together"* I Can't Have a Clean House While Raising Children *My Life Is Passing Me By* *I Am Responsible for My Child's Happiness* I Can't Do This Whole "Mothering Thing" *My Success as a Mom Is Directly Tied to How My Children Turn Out* I Don't Know What It Means to Be a Mom If I Only Have One Child *I Don't Have Time* My Postpartum Body Has to Look a Certain Way *Children Are a Nuisance and an Interruption* Children Are Really Expensive *Children Ruin a Marriage* My Focus Should Be on Rules and Regulations *The "Experts" Know Better How to Raise and Educate My Child Than I Do* The Most Important Thing Is My Child's Education *Good Moms Do "XYZ"* You Have to "Do" Motherhood the Way the Culture Tells You

LIE #12

I Am a Bad Mom

It's amazing how your terminology changes when you begin to allow the truths of God's Word to really alter how you think. This is especially true when it comes to the lie that we are bad moms. Natalie and Lena shared their struggles with this lie:

> [I believe] that I'm a bad mom. When my kids make mistakes this is the first place my mind goes.
>
> —Natalie

> [I believe] I'm a failure. Will I ever get this right?
>
> —Lena

Phylicia, a blogging friend of mine, recently inspired me through something she wrote to change the words I use to describe myself, reorienting them around the truth of the gospel. As she pointed out, the gospel changes our identity, and our words about ourselves need to reflect that change.

Here's what I mean: when we say we are bad moms, that description of ourselves is in direct contradiction to the gospel and its truth as to our new identity. If you say, "I am a bad mom" and then take "mom" off, what are you left with? "I am bad." Now, this may have been a very true characterization of yourself before you came to Christ when all your "righteousness" was still as filthy rags (Isaiah 64:6). However, it is no longer. Not because of some greatness in yourself, but because of the goodness that has been imputed to your account through the substitutionary atonement of Christ.

I have stated before in my writings in various places online that "I am an angry mom". However, I'm coming to see now that this is actually not true. Yes, I deal with anger issues at times, and mommy anger, in particular, is something I battle. But I am not an "angry mom". That is not who I am; it is not what constitutes my identity. What I am is a redeemed mom. I am a sinner, yes, but my story does not end there. I am a sinner saved by grace. As we have already seen when battling other lies, what I am is a new creation in Christ: "old things have passed away; behold, all things have become new" (2 Corinthians 5:17). My past (and present!) sins and struggles do not define me, dictate my identity, or make me who I am. Christ does. And He says I am a child of God (John 1:12), adopted into His family (Ephesians 1:5), accepted by Him (Romans 15:7), united with the Lord and one with Him in spirit (1 Corinthians 6:17), a chosen people, a holy nation, and His own special possession (1 Peter 2:9). That is who I am. I am no longer defined by my sin. If I think I am, then I am believing the gospel to be a lie, the atonement of Christ to be insufficient, and the old flesh to still be what is alive and ruling me.

Do not believe this lie, mama. If you are a child of God, if you have placed saving faith in Christ and what He did on the cross, you are a new creation—a creation no longer defined by sin. In fact, it is completely impossible for a Christian to be defined by sin or for a Christian mom to be defined as a "bad mom" because our sin has been removed as far as the east is from the west, completely forgotten by God. We need to begin truly believing that and allow it to begin affecting how we view ourselves in motherhood.

Part of the reason why it was so important for us to study where our identity is ultimately found (and to dispel the myth that we are to find our identity in being a mom), is because if we are finding our identity in motherhood, our worth will begin to be based on how good a job we are doing as moms. This will lead to our easily falling into the "I am a bad mom" trap when we sin and fall short. If, however, our identity is in Christ, our worth will be in the work He did, freeing us to walk in the salvation and newness He provided.

When you tell yourself you are a "bad mom", you are left with no inspiration to change, to grow, or to improve. You subconsciously think it impossible to do so because, after all, that is what you are—a bad mom (and we all know that a leopard can't change its spots). If, however, you go through your days of mothering telling yourself you are a redeemed and made-new mom, you will go through life with your head held high, your eyes fixed on Christ, and your heart filled with His power and love—all of which will result in a mom who is filled with hope as you are continuously being sanctified and made ever more into your Savior's image. Ultimately, that is the key—you have to take your eyes off your sin and instead plant them firmly on Him.

If you're worried about being a bad mom, take heart! That concern is evidence of the heart you have for your children, of the love you feel for them, and the desire you hold that you be the best you can possibly be for the little ones entrusted to your care. Then on those days when you sin against your children, let them down, hurt their feelings, and feel like a downright horrible mother, remember 1 John 2:1 which says, "These things I write to you, so that you may not sin. And if anyone sins, we have an Advocate with the Father, Jesus Christ the righteous."

Motherhood Is a Woman's Highest Calling *Mothering Is Unimportant Work* My Identity Is to Be Found in Being a Mother *I Am to Find My Ultimate Fulfillment in Motherhood* Mommy Guilt Is Just Something I Have to Live With *It's Wrong for Me to Go to God Again and Again After I Fail* Theology Isn't for Moms *I Have to Be a Perfect Mom* I Have to Do it All *I Am Enough* My Children Would Be Better Off Having a Different Mom *I'm a Bad Mom* I'm Selfish If I Have Any "Me Time" *I Need a Lot of "Me Time"* Motherhood Has to Be Hard (And Hard Is Bad!) *I Have to "Keep My Act Together"* I Can't Have a Clean House While Raising Children *My Life Is Passing Me By* *I Am Responsible for My Child's Happiness* I Can't Do This Whole "Mothering Thing" *My Success as a Mom Is Directly Tied to How My Children Turn Out* I Don't Know What It Means to Be a Mom If I Only Have One Child *I Don't Have Time* My Postpartum Body Has to Look a Certain Way *Children Are a Nuisance and an Interruption* Children Are Really Expensive *Children Ruin a Marriage* My Focus Should Be on Rules and Regulations *The "Experts" Know Better How to Raise and Educate My Child Than I Do* The Most Important Thing Is My Child's Education *Good Moms Do "XYZ"* You Have to "Do" Motherhood the Way the Culture Tells You

LIE #13

I'm Selfish If I Have Any "Me Time"

Oh, the dreaded topic of "me time"! In the hearts of moms everywhere, it produces equal parts anger, desperation, and frustration when we don't get it and guilt, remorse, and self-condemnation when we do. We just can't win! That is, unless we embrace the truth of God's Word instead of the expectations of man. Gerri and Amber share with us how they have bought into the lie that "me time" is selfish:

> [I've believed the lie that] you don't deserve "me" time or time alone with your spouse, that I'm a bad mom if I take time to myself to rest up and rejuvenate.
>
> —Gerri

> [I've believed the lie] that we don't have to care for ourselves.
>
> —Amber

If we are not always centering our time, attention, and work around our kiddos and their needs 24/7, we begin to feel guilty. This feeling of guilt stems from the lies we already addressed in the first part of this book:

that "motherhood is a woman's highest calling" and that "we are to find our identity and ultimate fulfillment in motherhood". The reality, though, is that this kind of thinking is doing our kids a great disservice. The fact of the matter is that children benefit little from having a mom who is always stressed out, angry, frustrated, frazzled, and overwhelmed. Additionally, the sobering reality is that if our daughters see us this way most of the time, they may begin thinking this is just what motherhood is all about, and not feel very inspired to ever want to be moms themselves. We need to be giving our kids the gift of a calm, peaceful, well-rested, and joyful mom which is only possible through the pursuit of rest, rejuvenation, time spent alone with the Lord, and, yes, the gift of "me time".

Jesus Prioritized "Me Time"

Throughout the Gospels, we find Jesus intentionally taking the time to separate Himself from the crowd and going off somewhere to be alone. For example:

> Now in the morning, having risen a long while before daylight, He went out and departed to a solitary place; and there He prayed. And Simon and those who were with Him searched for Him. When they found Him, they said to Him, "Everyone is looking for You." But He said to them, "Let us go into the next towns, that I may preach there also, because for this purpose I have come forth.
>
> —Mark 1: 35-38

There are several noteworthy aspects to this passage.

One is the fact that He, being omniscient, already knew everyone was looking for Him. He no doubt knew that the multitudes likely needed Him to answer questions, heal diseases, or mediate disagreements. This knowledge didn't mean that He immediately jumped up to go meet those needs, however. He knew that the most important thing He could do in those early moments of the day was first spend some time alone communing with the Father. In spite of the needs raging around Him, He intentionally took time to be alone, not putting it off until after everything else was done.

The second interesting thing is that He did not defend Himself to His disciples. When they finally found Christ and told Him they had been searching for Him, He didn't apologize for retreating to spend time alone.

Third, He understood that in order to fulfill the purpose for which He was sent (that of preaching the good news), He had to first prepare for that work by spending time with the Father. Doing so was not optional; it was a necessity. It was not a selfish use of time; it was preparation for the work set before Him.

> Immediately Jesus made His disciples get into the boat and go before Him to the other side, while He sent the multitudes away. And when He had sent the multitudes away, He went up on the mountain by Himself to pray. Now when evening came, He was alone there.
>
> —Matthew 14:22-23

This passage is incredibly noteworthy because it takes place directly following Christ's miraculous feeding of the five thousand. After such a never-before-seen miracle as providing nourishment to five thousand people with only five loaves of bread and two fish, there were undoubtedly folks there who were clamoring after Christ to perform more miracles, to heal them, to answer questions, and to fix problems. This is not what He did, however. He sent the people on their way, went out to a solitary place, and spent time alone with the Father:

> However, the report went around concerning Him all the more; and great multitudes came together to hear, and to be healed by Him of their infirmities. So He Himself often withdrew into the wilderness and prayed.
>
> —Luke 5:15-16

Did you catch that interesting wording there? "Great multitudes came .... *so* He Himself often withdrew." If we moms had been Jesus, the passage would have read something like this: "Great multitudes came, so He ran Himself ragged meeting every need, feeding every person, healing every injury and disease, answering every call, addressing every question or problem; and so, at the end of the day, He collapsed in exhaustion, wondering how He would live to face another day and dreading the fact that He would have to do it all over again tomorrow. Feeling so overwhelmed, He prayed in desperation as He drifted off to sleep—'Heaven help me if one of my disciples wakes me up in the middle of the night!'" Pretty big difference, huh? While this unique rendering of the passage seems rather humorous, it's actually quite sad if you think about it because of how accurately it represents the hearts of so many mamas.

The simple truth is that Jesus did not answer every person or meet every need. Yet we as moms somehow entertain the mistaken idea that we have to—as if we are better or more needed than Christ Himself. While we oftentimes view "me time" as being a selfish endeavor, it is clearly not sinful to spend time alone if the sinless Son of God made doing so a priority! How often, mamas, do we act as if we are omnipotent with no need for rest when even Christ Himself (who is truly omnipotent!)

did not act that way? Christ regularly made it His mission to rejuvenate Himself by spending time alone praying to the Father. Let's not make the mistake of thinking we are above having this same need ourselves.

God Prioritizes Rest

Jesus was not the first one to prioritize rest and refreshment. God the Father did so Himself from the very beginning and continues to do so to this day. After taking six days to bring all of creation into existence, He intentionally rested on the seventh day (Genesis 2:2-3). He later instituted the Sabbath which was made as a gift to man (Mark 2:27). We see in Hebrews 4 Jesus being described as our Sabbath rest: "There remains therefore a rest for the people of God. For he who has entered His rest has himself also ceased from his works as God did from His." (vs. 9-10). In Psalm 127 we read, "It is vain for you to rise up early, to sit up late, to eat the bread of sorrows; for so He gives His beloved sleep" (vs. 2). In Isaiah 30:15 God says, "In returning and rest you shall be saved; in quietness and confidence shall be your strength." Paul encourages us to "lead a quiet and peaceable life in all godliness and reverence" (1 Timothy 2:2). Clearly, it is God's desire for us as moms to embrace rest, quiet, solitude, and time alone when we can get it. And to not feel guilty for doing so! Because, in the end, making time for ourselves will fashion us into far better moms for our children.

How to Make "Me Time" a Reality

You may be a mama reading this right now feeling really discouraged. Perhaps you have three littles three and under, or maybe you have all teens who keep you up late at night talking and have you up early the next morning chauffeuring them all over town. Whatever your situation, maybe you are wondering how on earth you are supposed to find the time to be alone. The good news is there are far more options available to you when it comes to pursuing "me time" than this defeatist culture would have you think!

Make the Most of Nap Time (or Any Other Time Your Children Are Sleeping!)

I recently heard some of the best advice I've heard in a while: when your children are asleep, don't spend time doing things you can do when they are awake. I now don't do any of my cooking, cleaning, or other household chores when my children are sleeping. Those things are able to be accomplished when my little ones are awake and can then be brought alongside me and taught how those tasks are done. Instead, it is when my children are asleep that I have my quiet time, do my writing, get a lot of reading in, etc.—all of which fill me up and constitute as "me time".

Put Down the Phone

As much as I love social media and find that it can be harnessed to the glory of God and the advancement of His Kingdom, our smart phones, with all of the blogs, social media apps, and sources of entertainment they bring right to our fingertips are the bane of our existence in many ways. These little devices of technology which were designed to make our lives easier have actually sometimes made them worse. We are now duped into thinking we have no time for ourselves, no opportunity to do those things which fill us up, and no hope of rest or true refreshment, all because we spend all of our "free time" (and much time that isn't truly free!) scrolling on our phones. Just ask me how I know! If we took back even just a small portion of the time we have given over to staring at our phones (many times with nothing productive to show for it), and instead committed that time to doing those things which truly fill us up, we would discover just how much opportunity we actually have for "me time". The result would be radically different moms with amazingly transformed atmospheres in our homes.

Employ the Help of Grandma, Auntie, or Your Best Friend

Sometimes the easiest way to have time to yourself is to get a good friend from church or your child's grandma or aunt on board! Invite her over to spend some special one-on-one time with your little ones while you go out for some time to yourself. Your kids will be in good hands making precious memories, and you will come back refreshed and ready to take on another day.

Be Careful What You Spend Your "Me Time" Doing

In all of this discussion about the importance of "me time", how it is not at all selfish to sometimes take time to yourself, and how God actually expects us to do so, we do need to be careful how exactly we are filling that time alone when we have it. In order for it to truly make a difference, however, we have to make it count—really dedicating that time to doing those things which fill up our souls and provide lasting refreshment.

In the passages we studied above, Jesus didn't go off by Himself in order to seek entertainment or something empty and merely temporal (not that there isn't a time, on occasion, for a good show on Netflix or a nice manicure). He ultimately pursued refreshment that would last, that would build up His soul and gird Him with strength and comfort, equipping

Him for the work that was set before Him. He dedicated much of His time alone to communing with the Father, and so should we. Though doing so does not have to constitute all of our time spent alone, it should make up at least a portion of it.

Be encouraged today, mama, knowing that the Lord does not fault you for needing time to rest, to be rejuvenated, and to be built back up for the work to which you have been called. Jesus did those very things, and so should you.

LIE #14

I Need a Lot of "Me Time"

As we saw way back in the introduction, Satan is extra sneaky, tricking us into believing lies that are either on one extreme of the spectrum or the other. This is certainly true when it comes to the issue of "me time". On the one end of the spectrum we have his attempt at crippling us in our motherhood by believing the lie that pursuing "me time" is selfish. As soon as we are freed from that lie, however, he works double-time to re-enslave us by then blinding us with a lie from the opposite end of the spectrum: the lie that we need a lot of "me time". Suzanne and Aileen both made excellent points when they shared the following lies they have dealt with in their motherhood:

> [I have believed] the lie about needing so much "me-time". It's grounded in truth (we need to take care of our bodies and we also need to rest), but I think it has become an excuse to be selfish and do whatever we want.
>
> —Suzanne

> I wholeheartedly agree with [Suzanne]. We were blessed with children so we could teach them and show them

> the ways of the Lord and the world. Not to find ways to be without them.
>
> —Aileen

Whew, that's some hard truth there, right? But it is truth nevertheless, and we need to hear it. I have found this to be a problem in my own heart time and again. Being filled back up through self-care is definitely important—we can't pour out from an empty cup, after all. However, the problem comes, at least in my own selfish heart, when we begin viewing self-care as an all-out necessity. The end result is that we make that coveted me-time an idol.

This lie is particularly clever because, as Suzanne pointed out, it does find its roots in truth: that to take care of oneself is important. This is precisely how Satan likes to get us. He presents a lie that doesn't sound all that bad because it contains at least some truth. However, these seemingly innocuous lies are the hardest ones for us to reject precisely because of those bits of truth they contain.

What Are You Believing?

Being able to refute the lie that we require a ton of "me time" all comes down to what exactly we believe about our children, our God, and our life in general.

First, if we are viewing our children through the lens of lie #25, believing them to be nuisances and interruptions, then, of course, we are going to believe we require quite a bit of "me time". We are going to be feeling as if we have to get away from our children somehow, that our very life depends upon us being free from them even for just an afternoon. A desperation will begin to fester in our souls until we get that time away from our kids. If, however, we are viewing our children as the blessings and rewards they truly are (see Psalm 127:3-5), we will still have hard days in motherhood and will still need occasional time away (as we saw Jesus emulate when He went off to be apart from the crowd), but we won't be in all-out desperation for "me time" quite as often. If we understand that our children are eternal souls who have been entrusted into our care by Almighty God and not interruptions to "more important" pursuits, we will not, as Aileen put it, be so desperate to "find ways to be without them". It truly is all a matter of perspective.

The same goes for how we are viewing God. When the going gets tough in motherhood, and we are alternating between wanting to pull our hair out in frustration or cry our eyes out in exhaustion, our theology will affect how we view our situation and what we believe to be its remedy. If we have not been taking the time to study the attributes of God, have not been reading our Bibles or giving any attention to the study of theology, it will be easy to fall into the trap of making "me time" into an idol, believing it to be the ultimate answer to our motherhood problems. If, however, we are students of theology, having understood its importance and seen how very applicable it is to our lives as moms, then we will know that God is all we truly need. He is all-sufficient, able to meet our every need, able to fill us up when the going gets tough and we can't get a break, and able to strengthen and sustain us through all of life's hard days. The truth of the matter is this: ultimately, we don't need even more "me time". We need more Jesus. We need to fix our eyes firmly on Him, for doing so will instantly begin to drown out our troubles, making them seem not quite so big after all.

This is also where the truth of Philippians 4:13 is so applicable. Throughout the context surrounding verse 13, Paul is sharing with the church at Philippi what some of his struggles and hardships have been. He says that he knows what it's like to be hungry and what it's like to be full, he has experienced both great need as well as great abundance, and, through it all, he has learned to be content. That is when he then pens those popular words: "I can do all things through Christ who strengthens me".

Therefore, Philippians 4:13 is all about being able to endure any hardship or trial that comes our way; it's about being content in the life we have been given. This is precisely why it is such a relevant passage for moms who are struggling with the difficulties and challenges motherhood brings. Paul doesn't say, "I can do all things once I first have an hour of me time alone at the coffee shop." He doesn't say, "I can do all things through the strength given me through a refreshing time at the mall." He doesn't say, "I can do all things as long as I first get my manicure." No. He says, "I can do all things through Christ who strengthens me."

These examples of what the verse does not say may seem rather humorous and outlandish—of course Paul didn't write it that way! Unfortunately, as silly as they may seem, they are nevertheless quite representative of what we sometimes believe to be true. We take "me time" and change it from the legitimately beneficial pursuit it is into an all-out necessity, when the fact of the matter is all we need is Christ. As much as I love my coffee and think those shirts that say *All I need is Jesus and coffee*! are cute, they aren't telling us the truth. In fact, they are subtly feeding us a lie. All we need is the Lord. Ultimately, He is the only one who can eternally sustain us when the going gets tough. Coffee, shopping, peace and quiet, and manicures may all build us up momentarily, but the feelings of refreshment brought about by those temporal pursuits don't last. Only one thing does, and that is our relationship with the Lord and the life-sustaining power He gives.

This is precisely why Satan works double-time to get us to believe this lie in the first place. If he can get our eyes off Christ and onto the belief that "me time" is the quintessential need of every mom, he can succeed in weakening us in our motherhood and render us lacking in vision, purpose, strength, and vigor for the task set before us. True strength for mothering comes not through mocha lattes and nail polish. It comes from the Lord as a result of being in close relationship with Him. This is precisely why we need to follow the example of Christ, being sure to incorporate communion with the Father into any alone time we may have.

The last thing I want to point out in regards to this lie is something that will directly carry us over into the next lie we will be addressing and that is this: we need to stop expecting life to be easy and then having a hissy fit when it isn't. I'm speaking to myself here because there is nothing that sends me into a tailspin of frustration, revealing the selfishness that resides in my heart, more than a diaper blowout occurring right when I'm running late for an outing, or a baby refusing to take a nap when I want him to, or a little one waking up unexpectedly. In those moments, I don't need to run from the challenge by making a beeline for the nearest coffee shop to get in some time alone. I need to face the situation head-on, relying on God my Savior for the strength to address the challenge with selfless love, grace, warmth, and patient endurance. That will make more of a difference in my attitude and my ability to be the kind of mom my kids need than any "me time" ever could!

Motherhood Is a Woman's Highest Calling *Mothering Is Unimportant Work* My Identity Is to Be Found in Being a Mother *I Am to Find My Ultimate Fulfillment in Motherhood* Mommy Guilt Is Just Something I Have to Live With *It's Wrong for Me to Go to God Again and Again After I Fail* Theology Isn't for Moms *I Have to Be a Perfect Mom* I Have to Do it All *I Am Enough* My Children Would Be Better Off Having a Different Mom *I'm a Bad Mom* I'm Selfish If I Have Any "Me Time" *I Need a Lot of "Me Time"* Motherhood Has to Be Hard (And Hard Is Bad!) *I Have to "Keep My Act Together"* I Can't Have a Clean House While Raising Children *My Life Is Passing Me By* *I Am Responsible for My Child's Happiness* I Can't Do This Whole "Mothering Thing" *My Success as a Mom Is Directly Tied to How My Children Turn Out* I Don't Know What It Means to Be a Mom If I Only Have One Child *I Don't Have Time* My Postpartum Body Has to Look a Certain Way *Children Are a Nuisance and an Interruption* Children Are Really Expensive *Children Ruin a Marriage* My Focus Should Be on Rules and Regulations *The "Experts" Know Better How to Raise and Educate My Child Than I Do* The Most Important Thing Is My Child's Education *Good Moms Do "XYZ"* You Have to "Do" Motherhood the Way the Culture Tells You

LIE #15

Motherhood Has to Be Hard (And Hard Is Bad!)

If you were to describe many of today's moms, what words would you use? The first ones that come to my mind are stressed, overly busy, overwhelmed, frustrated, tired, martyrs, victims, and downtrodden. It's not a very encouraging list, is it? Unfortunately, though, it is an accurate representation of the kinds of things you hear older moms say to women who are pregnant with their first babies:

> Oh, just wait—you won't believe how much work you are in for!
>
> Enjoy your sleep while you can still get it.
>
> Enjoy your freedom—it'll soon be gone.
>
> You'll never shower again!
>
> Your days of being able to go to the bathroom alone are numbered.

It's pretty shocking the kind of victim mentality and discouraging words that are put forward to women these days who are simply excited about having a baby and becoming a mom. Several ladies wrote in to share their experiences with these kinds of lies:

> [A common lie] is that it's okay to feel like you're drowning and failing all the time because that's just "how moms feel".
>
> —Lauren Jane

> [People say] you'll never have a full night's sleep again. My kids sleep 7-7. Or [they say] your life is over, say goodbye to your romantic life and your sleep. Really?? Says who?? Plan dates, make an effort to keep the spark!
>
> —Jessica

> [I've believed that] motherhood has to be hard!
>
> —Brittany

Is it true that motherhood can be challenging, that the transition to becoming a mom is one that is fraught with growing pains, that the role of mom stretches you, exposing in startling ways the sin and selfishness which reside in your heart, and that the work of mothering is used by God to sanctify you? Absolutely! Acknowledging the challenges that motherhood brings is a far cry, however, from the kind of victim mentality (which Satan inspires) possessed by many a mom these days.

As we have already seen more than once throughout the course of this book, the Lord wants more for us than the kind of joyless martyr-complex we sometimes have the tendency to take upon ourselves. He has made us more than conquerors (Romans 8:37) in the face of tribulation, distress, famine, and any other kind of hardship we may face in this life (vs. 36). The Greek word translated as "more than conquerors" is hypernikaō, which literally means "to vanquish beyond, to gain a decisive victory:—more than conquer."[16]

Do we believe we can "gain a decisive victory" over the lies of Satan which work to bring us down? Do we believe we can vanquish the feelings of discouragement which come from the challenging days of motherhood? The truth is that we don't have to give in, viewing ourselves as victims to motherhood. We don't have to feel, as Lauren said, "like we're failing all the time". Not if we believe that we have been given all the strength (Philippians 4:13), power (Romans 8:11), and help (Psalm 121:2) we could ever need through Christ and the Holy Spirit. Not if we believe that Christ came so that we could have abundant life even in the midst of Satan's attempts to steal, kill, and destroy (John 10:10). And not if we believe that the hard things are often the good things.

In our culture of ease and comfort, we hate for things to be hard. If we struggle with the hard seasons of life or face challenging pushback in what we have set out to do, we quickly give up. If something turns out to be hard, we think we erred and made a wrong choice. If only we were more like the Americans of yesteryear such as Thomas Edison who failed hundreds of times before succeeding in his various inventions; the beloved Dr. Seuss whose first book was rejected by twenty-seven different publishers; or Henry Ford who had two failed business attempts in the automobile industry (and two subsequent bankruptcies!), but refused to give up, going on to design the model T, the assembly line, and the powerhouse that we all know today as the Ford Motor Company. If we moms possessed even just a hint of their grit and determination, imagine how it would revolutionize how we approach the hard seasons of motherhood!

The ironic thing is though we may not possess the kind of determination those great men had, we actually possess something far greater and more powerful: the Holy Spirit of God Himself. And yet we act as if we have no hope, as if we have no choice but to allow the hard moments of motherhood to drown us in self-pity and desperation. When older moms say to newer ones, "Oh just wait until your baby is born…", it's not merely a case of bad timing or a discouraging thing for an expectant mama to hear. It also stems from a defeatist attitude that can then become a self-fulfilling prophecy. If you believe you have to be a victim of motherhood, you likely will be. Motherhood does not have to turn us into victims, however. Is mothering hard? Yes, sometimes it is. Is it challenging, sometimes stretching us to the core? Yes. But anything worthwhile often is.

It is because "hard" does not equal "fun" or "blissful" or "happy" that we think it must equal "bad". But what we have to come to grips with is the fact that "hard" does not equal "bad". As much as hard times hurt as they are growing us, they are nevertheless doing just that—growing us ever more into the image of Christ. More growth occurs during the hard times than in any other season of our lives. Romans 5:3-5 says, "We also glory in tribulations, knowing that tribulation produces perseverance; and perseverance, character; and character, hope. Now hope does not disappoint, because the love of God has been poured out in our hearts by the Holy Spirit who was given to us." According to this order of things, if we are approaching hardship with the viewpoint of God, girded by His love, and understanding that He brings good out of all things (Romans 8:28), then any tribulation we face will result in perseverance, character, and, ultimately, unwavering hope. James confirmed this teaching of Paul's when he wrote, "My brethren, count it all joy when you fall into various trials, knowing that the testing of your faith produces patience. But let patience have its perfect work, that you may be perfect and complete, lacking nothing" (James 1:2-4).

What a different perspective this is from the one common in our culture which believes a trial to be something that is discouraging and steals your life away. The gospel perspective is one that says we are to count it all joy when we face various trials because we know what the wonderful end result of those trials will be in us: strength of character, patience, and a woman who is thoroughly perfected, completed, and equipped for this life and the life to come. Trials are used by God to fashion us into women who lack nothing, but who realize we already have everything we could ever need in Christ and the abundant life He brings. True joy comes from knowing who we are and what we have in Christ, which is precisely why we are able to take joy in seasons of trial. It is those very seasons which serve to open our eyes ever more to the truth of our loving Lord and what He has done for us.

What do we do, though, when we are just having one of "those" days? When we feel like Laura has felt when she wrote in and said, "I hate hearing that I have to enjoy every moment with [my children] while they are little because I know time is fleeting, but some days and moments are just plain difficult, and I want nothing more than the fresh start of a new day." This is when we again need to take every thought captive to the obedience of Christ and look to the Word for the hope and help that we need. God understands our feelings. He knows all about the challenges of motherhood that we face (after all, He faced several similar challenges like sleep deprivation and the never-ending needs of others throughout His earthly ministry). It is precisely because of those moments when we just want the day to be over and to have a reset that the Lord graciously included a passage in His Word that says, "Through the Lord's mercies we are not consumed, because His compassions fail not. They are new every morning; Great is Your faithfulness" (Lamentations 3:22-23).

So often I think we moms buy into the lie that we must be experiencing happiness in motherhood at all times or else we must not love our kids. There is a difference, however, between happiness and joy. Joy is a fruit of the Spirit (Galatians 5:22), a direct result of the Lord's work in our hearts, and stems from us keeping our focus squarely on the good gews of the gospel. Happiness, on the other hand, is circumstantial and conditional. If we are not exceedingly giddy and happy in our motherhood at every moment, it is not evidence that we don't love our kids; it's evidence that we still have a sin nature, that we still have the old flesh, and that we still need the strength of Christ on a moment-by-moment basis. It is evidence that we still struggle with selfishness, pride, and a wrong perspective of hardship. Our story, however, does not have to end there!

Motherhood Is Hard...and It's Good!

So, is motherhood hard? Yes. That part is no lie! Anytime something requires as much sacrifice and selflessness as motherhood, it's going to be hard. It is a lie, however, to believe that hard equals bad or to believe that motherhood has to be hard in the kind of defeatist, discouraging ways described by Lauren, Jessica, and many other moms in our day. The common posts on Facebook that tell us motherhood means never getting any sleep, never having meaningful conversations with our husbands, never having any time to ourselves, never eating a decent hot meal, and never having a clean house are lying to us. Do we honestly think that God would design something as beautiful as motherhood—even as touched by the curse as it may now be—and allow it to be so grueling that we have no other alternative but to become victims under it? If we are buying into this lie, it is because we are believing a far worse lie at the foundation of it all: that God does not desire for us to thrive, to live in abundant joy and peace, or to operate from a place of strength with the help and fortitude He provides.

While we know that life is sometimes hard thanks to the fall, the curse, and our sin nature, we must likewise remember that God has redeemed it, which means "hard" does not have to equal "bad". Just think of it—Christ dying on the cross sure seemed to be the epitome of bad, but look at where we would be without that saving sacrifice! Our God is in the business of redeeming all things, causing everything to work together for the good of His children (see Romans 8:28). Remember that, sweet mama, the next time you are up at all hours of the night with your newborn or dealing with another toddler temper tantrum. Remember those hard times are used to fashion you more and more into the likeness of Christ. Nothing could be better than that!

Motherhood Is a Woman's Highest Calling *Mothering Is Unimportant Work* My Identity Is to Be Found in Being a Mother *I Am to Find My Ultimate Fulfillment in Motherhood* Mommy Guilt Is Just Something I Have to Live With *It's Wrong for Me to Go to God Again and Again After I Fail* Theology Isn't for Moms *I Have to Be a Perfect Mom* I Have to Do it All *I Am Enough* My Children Would Be Better Off Having a Different Mom *I'm a Bad Mom* I'm Selfish If I Have Any "Me Time" *I Need a Lot of "Me Time"* Motherhood Has to Be Hard (And Hard Is Bad!) *I Have to "Keep My Act Together"* I Can't Have a Clean House While Raising Children *My Life Is Passing Me By* *I Am Responsible for My Child's Happiness* I Can't Do This Whole "Mothering Thing" *My Success as a Mom Is Directly Tied to How My Children Turn Out* I Don't Know What It Means to Be a Mom If I Only Have One Child *I Don't Have Time* My Postpartum Body Has to Look a Certain Way *Children Are a Nuisance and an Interruption* Children Are Really Expensive *Children Ruin a Marriage* My Focus Should Be on Rules and Regulations *The "Experts" Know Better How to Raise and Educate My Child Than I Do* The Most Important Thing Is My Child's Education *Good Moms Do "XYZ"* You Have to "Do" Motherhood the Way the Culture Tells You

LIE #16

I Have to "Keep My Act Together"

The exact wording of this lie came from Faith, who shared that this is what she struggles with the most in her mothering. It's a belief that, at least in part, stems from another lie that was sent in by Ellie:

> I assume other mamas are judging me 100% of the time. I also struggle with believing that I'm doing enough for my son (again, because of judgement or assumed judgement).

The belief that as a mom I have to "keep my act together" is one Satan likes to use particularly because it adversely affects so many areas of our lives: from keeping us from building close friendships with other moms to believing ourselves to be failures in God's eyes if we don't do everything perfectly. It's pretty easy to see how this lie directly contradicts the truths and priorities of the gospel. Where exactly does the lie come from, though? We know Satan conceived it, but how does he get us to believe it in the first place? I see three main problem areas which lead to our believing that we have to keep our acts together, and they are as follows:

Comparison

The comparison game is so ugly and never produces any winners. Either we are always looking down our noses at other moms who "don't have it as together as we do", or else we are downtrodden and discouraged, feeling that we are not living up to the facade we have built in our minds of what other moms out there are doing. Either way, comparison breeds disunity, hurt feelings, pride, discouragement, and walls around our hearts which can be very hard to break down. It also leads to the belief that we have to keep our acts together.

After all, if we are in the business of comparing, we most likely don't want to come up short and be found wanting when other moms compare themselves to us. And thus, the vicious cycle continues of being in bondage to comparison and attempting to have it all together. We need to remember what the gospel has to say about this (because, yes, it is so applicable that it is relevant even to this struggle!). The gospel reminds us that "there is none righteous, no, not one...there is none who does good, no, not one" (Romans 3:10, 12). We are all on an equal playing field in God's eyes, with no one being better or worse than someone else. Prior to salvation, all our "good works" are as filthy rags (Isaiah 64:6); and following the moment of salvation, all believers are clothed in the righteousness of Christ, rendering the comparison game irrelevant. There is but one comparison game we should ever be engaging in, and that is comparing ourselves to Christ, seeking to imitate Him and live more as He did (Ephesians 5:1).

Perfectionism

This one goes right along with the comparison problem and oftentimes produces the same icky fruit. When we think we are achieving perfection ourselves, we can easily fall into the trap of pride and a Pharisaical attitude which looks down its nose at other moms. When we are expecting perfection in others, we then begin judging other moms for failing to live up to our own man-made expectations. I don't know about you, but I would have a hard time breaking free from the belief that I have to keep my act together if the spirit of perfectionism is around!

A Lack of Vulnerability

This is an awkward and sometimes painful area to deal with at first. However, if we want to be free from the exhausting burden of thinking we have to keep our act together, then we are going to have to be vulnerable. If we want to be the kind of friend our sisters-in-Christ can come to with their deepest and darkest secrets, struggles, and sins, knowing they will hear words of wisdom, truth, and love spoken over them as well as find a shoulder to cry on, then we are going to have to be honest about our own struggles. We are going to have to work to cultivate a spirit of transparency and open honesty among Christian women. No one is going to feel comfortable enough to open up to us about the fact that they don't have it all together unless they first know we are a safe place for them to let down their guard and end their mirage of perfection. The only way we will prove ourselves as that safe place for them is if we, too, admit we aren't perfect, that we understand their struggles because we have struggles of our own, if we share with them the sins that so easily entangle us, and if we go first in showing we don't have our acts together. In doing so, we will be able to faithfully "bear one another's burdens (Galatians 6:2)" and lift one another up, spurring each other on in our walks with the Lord.

The Remedy

For each of these three common starting points which leads to the development of the "I have to keep it all together" mentality, there is but one remedy we need, and that is time in the Word.

To end the comparison game, we have to study the Word and discover that we have no business comparing ourselves to each other, for we are all fellow sinners. Our sole focus instead ought to be comparing ourselves to Christ and asking ourselves how we can go about living more and more as He did.

To abandon perfectionism, we have to study the Word in an effort to look to Christ and understand that it is His righteousness that we have already had imparted to us through our faith in Him. The pursuit of perfection then becomes a silly one for a Christian. On the one hand, we have already been made perfect in God's eyes. But on the other hand, we know we will never be sinless on this side of heaven. Thus, rather than tirelessly pursuing the empty god of perfectionism, we need to instead be simply imitating Christ as best we can through the strength He gives.

To embrace vulnerability, we have to know the Word and the condition of our sinful hearts in comparison to it. We need to then open up to others, share our sins and struggles, and, in so doing, build true, lasting, deep friendships where iron will sharpen iron and where we will be able to bear one another's burdens and point each other to Christ.

Why Satan Wants You to Put on an Act

Have you ever wondered exactly how Satan thrives through getting us to believe we have to "keep our act together"? Note the wording and you'll see why: he wants us to keep our "act" together. He wants us to be acting. Satan does not want us to ever be real, open, or honest. Again, his focus is on deception. He can't stand for people to know, embrace, or share the truth. In fact, I believe Satan has four main objectives that he is setting out to accomplish by getting us to present facades of perfection to others:

1. He wants to silence our witness.

If Satan can convince us that we had better keep our acts together, he can then be successful in his mission to silence our Christian witness and keep us from pointing others to Christ. It is only when we are actually open and honest about our sinful pasts and how God has taken us from darkness to light (Ephesians 5:8) that we are able to put the redeeming power of God on full display. Likewise, it is only when we share openly about our present struggles with sin and our tendency to still fall short that we can also share about God's strength that is made perfect in our weakness (2 Corinthians 12:9), the comforting realization that God will never leave us nor forsake us (Deuteronomy 31:8), and the fact that His love for us never changes (Romans 8:31-39). Our testimonies are what serve to both point the lost to Christ as well as encourage those already in the faith. It is no wonder then that Satan is working overtime to silence them.

The enemy of our souls likes to whisper to us that if people ever knew the real us and the real sins and struggles we face on a daily basis, they would never want anything to do with the God whose name we claim. He wants us to believe that if we share about how we struggle with sin and temptation, we will somehow tarnish God and sully His reputation. Nothing could be further from the truth, though. In fact, it is precisely in hearing those powerful redemption stories like that of the Apostle Paul or John Newton that our faith is built and our trust in the God of the Bible is strengthened. We need to quit acting as if we have it all together and instead point folks to the God who does! We'll see their faith, as well as our own, built up in the process.

2. He wants to stunt our growth.

We all know that nagging someone, continuously harping on a person's sins and failures, does little to inspire that person to greatness. The same goes for us, and Satan knows this. Have you ever thought, I *must be such a failure—everyone else has their act together far better than I do,* or *No one struggles like I do,* or *I'll never get this right—all I do is fail; just imagine if everyone knew the real me*? These are the kind of discouraging thoughts that invade our minds when we believe Satan's lie that we must keep our act together. When everyone else seems perfect (because they have believed this lie themselves), we begin to despair. When we feel the pressure to be perfect and never let anyone down, we become discouraged. What ends up happening at that point is we feel as if we will never measure up, so we begin to give up. We have to be inspired to greatness in order to pursue greatness. If all we ever think on are lies of condemnation and hopelessness, we will soon, little by little, give up in our quest to imitate Christ.

3. He wants to keep us lonely and isolated.

You have to be perfect for people to like you.

People wouldn't want anything to do with you if they knew who you really are.

You had better not let your sin show.

You can't be completely real with that person—what would they think of you?

Have you ever entertained such thoughts? It was not by accident that these seeds of doubt and discouragement seeped into your mind. Satan is always on a mission to keep you alone and isolated, cut off from the encouragement of solid Christian friends who will help you up when you fall (Ecclesiastes 4:10). As we saw above, where there is no vulnerability there is no close Christian friendship because we don't feel free to share with others; they, likewise, do not feel that they can let down their guard and share with us. If Satan can isolate us in our Christian walk, he can render us far weaker and more ineffective in our attempts to spread the gospel than we otherwise would be with supportive friends by our side.

4. He wants to continue this vicious cycle with our children and our communities.

The sobering thing is that our beliefs—which always end up directly affecting how we live—have a big impact on our children as they grow. This can be a great thing if we are believing (and then living out) solid Biblical truth. If we are embracing Satan's lies, however, chances are good that our children will, as well. What we have to remember is that when we believe we have to keep our act together, our children will grow up thinking the same is true for them. The cycle will continue, with successive generations becoming weaker and weaker in their understanding of the gospel and its full implications for daily living.

The same could be said of our churches and communities at large. If we keep living the lie that says we have it all together, chances are others will, as well. The truth is that someone has to go first if a change is to be made. The mistake we make is in expecting that "someone" to be the other person when, really, change begins with us. Giving ourselves permission to let down our guard, to be real and vulnerable, and to expose our need for Christ through our imperfections will inspire others to do the same.

When we understand that we no longer have to keep our act together (and that, truly, the reach of the gospel is far greater when we don't), we will begin to experience a freedom we may have never felt before. It will be the freedom which comes from knowing we can be real, open, and honest. It will be the freedom to consistently point others to Christ through our imperfections and His sanctifying power. The result will be that kind of beautiful, faithful friendship and community that we all crave. And, you know what? It will be so worth the work it required to get there!

So, mama, you no longer have to tirelessly strive to keep your act together—you have Christ to lean on instead. He will give you the hope and peace for which your soul longs.

LIE #17

I Can't Have a Clean House While Raising Children

I think it's time for some real talk, mamas. I've shot straight with you already when addressing the first sixteen lies in this book, but things are about to get really vulnerable. So, here is the truth:

My name is Rebekah Hargraves, and oftentimes I really struggle to keep a clean home.

You're shocked, right? I mean, what mom ever struggles with keeping her house clean? Clearly, I'm saying this in jest because we have all seen the hundred and one memes floating around Facebook that say things like: "Good moms have sticky floors" and "Trying to clean your house while raising kids is like trying to brush your teeth while eating Oreos." What may surprise you is not that I struggle in this area, but what two women shared regarding what they view as one of the most common lies they see moms embracing today:

> [I always hear] 'You can only have one of two things: clean floors or happy kids.' I literally HATE that line! It implies that caring for your home and keeping a clean house are mutually exclusive with happy kids, which is

> not only a lie, but often used as an excuse not to make an effort at home.
>
> —Phylicia

> I so often hear the lie that, if you are raising children, your house can never be clean. I am a mother of 12, and I can tell you—that is not the case!
>
> —Chrissy

Now, hear me out, mama! Don't close the book at this point because you struggle in the area of homemaking. Don't skip this chapter because you may have bought into the lie that having a clean house is an impossibility, and you are now worried you might be judged as a result of the current condition of your home. That is not what is going to happen here, as I have no desire to heap guilt and judgment onto your shoulders. For one thing, considering my own struggle, it would be hypocritical judgment! We have already seen how harsh negativity does very little to inspire someone to greatness. So instead, I want to cast a vision for you of the importance of home and all that goes on within that sphere and, in so doing, encourage you in your efforts to craft a clean, welcoming home.

The truth is that this is not about having a perfectly spotless home, every last inch of which could pass the white glove test. This is about embracing the opportunity and the responsibility we have been given to form and fashion a place in which love and care will be shown, laughter and tears will be shared, and hearts and souls will be touched for the Kingdom.

Can all of that happen in a messy home? Certainly, it can. The homemaker, however, will find herself feeling far more stressed and her environment far less peaceful and inviting. After all, excessive messiness has never been known for being very conducive to hospitality!

How the Gospel Pertains to Cleaning Your House

At this point, you may be wondering what the gospel could possibly have to do with this area of homemaking. I want to encourage you with the truth that because God's Word is applicable to each and every aspect of life, that includes the aspect of cleaning your house!

As I've already mentioned once before, Emily Jensen and Laura Wifler from the Risen Motherhood Podcast make it their mission to apply the gospel to even the most seemingly unimportant or smallest details of daily life. In fact, Laura was recently interviewed on another podcast[17] where she talked about home decor and how the gospel relates to even that area of homemaking. It was inspiring to hear how even crafting your home decor can be a picture of God and how He creates and values beauty. I propose today that as with home decor, household chores can also point to the truth and beauty of the gospel.

If you have ever been to the Creation Museum run by Answers in Genesis, then you have likely noticed how they describe the good news of the gospel using the "Seven C's": "Creation, Corruption, Catastrophe, Confusion, Christ, Cross, Consummation". When you take a messy, chaotic, disorganized home and fashion it into a place of order, organization, and harmony, you can use that transformation as an illustration for your children of the gospel and what it accomplished. When our homes are messy, they present a picture of the curse and its results—chaos, disorder, and confusion. When you then clean your home, you are able to tangibly show your children what Christ accomplished on the cross and what will ultimately occur at the end of time—order restored. Isn't that neat? When even seemingly simple tasks like cleaning the floors or organizing a closet can point us and our children to the Lord, they become far less "mundane" and don't feel as much like drudgery. Instead, even our household tasks are able to be viewed as important and full of purpose.

As many of us can attest, when our homes are in disarray and everything is dirty or a mess, we do not feel at peace. We feel anxious, stressed out, and overwhelmed. This is not by accident. I believe this is a direct result of our having been made in the image of a God who is a God of order (1 Corinthians 14:33). He is a God who desires that "all things be done decently and in order" (1 Corinthians 14:40). Deep down, I believe this is true of us, as well (even for those of us who are not as type-A in personality and can actually still thrive under a little chaos!).

In addition to the idea of cleaning and organizing your home as being work that reflects the gospel, it is work that also aids us in our mission to spread the gospel. Hospitality is a very impactful tool for reaching people for Christ, and, chances are, you are only going to want to extend hospitality to guests if your home is not a total pigsty. We tend to have one standard of cleanliness we find acceptable in our own homes when just our families are around, but quite another when it comes to having guests. If that is the case for you, make it your mission to do one or two little tasks a day that will make it possible for your home to largely be in that condition on a daily basis, ready for you to be able to practice hospitality at the drop of a hat. Upkeep is so much easier than overhaul (just ask me how I know!). So, if you do little things on a daily basis (such as make sure the dishes are done and the living room is picked up before you go to bed) and slightly larger tasks on a weekly basis (such as cleaning the bathrooms or tending to the floors), you will greatly reduce your stress level and increase the cleanliness of your home. In reality, no individual household chore takes all that long to do—throwing in a load of laundry and folding another load, mopping the floor, and cleaning the bathroom are each tasks which do not take large blocks of time to complete. There truly is hope for a clean home, mama! Even when you're busy raising children.

I know what you are likely thinking, though. You see that there is time for the household tasks at hand, but you have a bunch of little people in your life. You have discovered that each of these little people has the superpower of, in a matter of minutes, being able to completely obliterate the work it took you an hour to do. Therefore, you are tempted to give up, throw your hands up in defeat, and think, *What's the point?* I'll tell you what the point is—the point is that you are a parent, and, as such, it is your responsibility to train and instruct your children in the character qualities of having a good work ethic, never giving up, and believing in the importance of doing the work God has given you to do no matter what the outcome may be.

Is it sometimes hard to get household duties done when you have little ones who like to get into things? Of course, it is! That doesn't mean we have to just give up, however. Instead, it means we bring those little ones alongside us, taking full advantage of the desire they tend to have at those young ages to help and capitalizing on their uncanny ability to learn. It means we train them into little workers in their own right who see the value in hard work, delight in a job well done, and understand the importance of working together as a family unit to keep the family home in good shape. Cultivating a clean and welcoming home not only blesses our families and guests, but it is also a way by which we are able to train our children in the importance of this aspect of homemaking. If we are giving up on being able to have a clean home because we are in the season of raising children, we are missing out—and so are our kids.

The common lie Phylicia shared about our choice as moms being between having clean floors or happy children is representative of a false dichotomy. It is as if we believe that cleaning our homes means we are taking time away from our kids or prohibiting them from playing and enjoying their childhood. First, if we view dedicating time to cleaning as stealing time from our children, we may be doing it wrongly. We may be forgetting that they can come alongside us and help us clean (and have a chat with us in the process!). Second, if cleaning our homes is stealing childhood joy from our kiddos, then we are likely doing something wrong here, as well. We have either run too far to the opposite extreme of believing everything must be perfectly clean, perfectly picked up, perfectly spotless at all times (which will definitely steal the joy of the other folks in our home), or else we are viewing cleaning as drudgery rather than the opportunity it could be for fostering friendship and closeness with our children as we work side by side.

Granted, especially when our kiddos are little and oftentimes getting into things, it can be hard at times to keep the house together. And there is abundant grace for those days when our house is a mess—remember, this is not about making a clean home into an idol. We do need to keep first things first and practice proper priorities. If we find ourselves cleaning and organizing our homes more than we find ourselves reading to our little ones or spending time with our husbands, something does need to change, and we do need to keep our priorities from getting out of whack. However, we likewise still need to remember that working towards cultivating a clean and welcoming home, both for our family who lives there and for those guests we invite in, is an important and worthwhile pursuit. Just as the Proverbs 31 woman did, we should be dedicating our time to watching over the ways of our households and not eating the bread of idleness (vs. 27), while at the same time being careful to do our husbands good (vs. 12) and so love and tend to our children that they would desire to rise up and call us blessed (vs. 28).

The hard truth is this: I have found that, for me, if I don't have a clean house it isn't because my children are preventing me from having one. It's because I have instead chosen to spend my time on empty pursuits such as idly scrolling through social media. We need to stop blaming our children for our tendency towards laziness. Instead, we need to seek God's help for our problem. We need to grow in this area and, in so doing, work towards keeping our children from the trap of idleness, as well. We need to instill in them a delight in a job well done and a desire to properly care for those things—such as our homes and other possessions—which the Lord has called us to steward well. The truth of the matter is you can keep a reasonably clean home while at the same time raising children. The question is: do you want to?

Motherhood Is a Woman's Highest Calling *Mothering Is Unimportant Work* My Identity Is to Be Found in Being a Mother *I Am to Find My Ultimate Fulfillment in Motherhood* Mommy Guilt Is Just Something I Have to Live With *It's Wrong for Me to Go to God Again and Again After I Fail* Theology Isn't for Moms *I Have to Be a Perfect Mom* I Have to Do it All *I Am Enough* My Children Would Be Better Off Having a Different Mom *I'm a Bad Mom* I'm Selfish If I Have Any "Me Time" *I Need a Lot of "Me Time"* Motherhood Has to Be Hard (And Hard Is Bad!) *I Have to "Keep My Act Together"* I Can't Have a Clean House While Raising Children *My Life Is Passing Me By* *I Am Responsible for My Child's Happiness* I Can't Do This Whole "Mothering Thing" *My Success as a Mom Is Directly Tied to How My Children Turn Out* I Don't Know What It Means to Be a Mom If I Only Have One Child *I Don't Have Time* My Postpartum Body Has to Look a Certain Way *Children Are a Nuisance and an Interruption* Children Are Really Expensive *Children Ruin a Marriage* My Focus Should Be on Rules and Regulations *The "Experts" Know Better How to Raise and Educate My Child Than I Do* The Most Important Thing Is My Child's Education *Good Moms Do "XYZ"* You Have to "Do" Motherhood the Way the Culture Tells You

LIE #18

My Life Is Passing Me By

It's hard to transition to being a mom. It's a season full of growing pains! You go from being able to make up your own schedule and doing what you want to do when you want to do it, to having a little person largely dictate what happens and at what time (especially in those early days!). It can be easy sometimes to covet the freedom your non-mama friends have to pursue dreams or plan vacations or enjoy girl time at the drop of a hat. This is why it is so important to recognize and refute the lie Summer shared with us:

> [A lot of moms believe] that their life is passing them by, rather than embracing/understanding that their lives aren't passing them by, but rather will just look different in this season. Sometimes they believe that joy is only before and after raising littles, when in reality, joy can be found in the middle of the day to day of our newfound calling.
>
> —Summer

I love the truth Summer shared with us there! What a perfect way to combat what has become a terribly common lie these days: the lie that if you are a mom, your life is passing you by. If we were to truly grasp the importance of motherhood and understand how it impacts the world, we wouldn't be feeling as if our lives are passing us by while we are in the season of mothering. Instead, we would be feeling as if we were on the adventure of a lifetime, directly affecting the course of human history itself! For that is the true nature of what we are doing. William Ross Wallace beautifully captured this truth in his poem, "The Hand that Rocks the Cradle is the Hand that Rules the World." Here is one stanza:

Woman, how divine your mission
Here upon our natal sod!
Keep, oh, keep the young heart open
Always to the breath of God!
All true trophies of the ages
Are from mother-love impearled;
For the hand that rocks the cradle
Is the hand that rules the world.[18]

If that doesn't fire you up for the work of mothering, I don't know what will! Please understand, dear mama, that your life is not passing you by. Christ came that we might have abundant life (John 10:10), and, while that certainly pertains to the eternal life we have to look forward to, it describes what He desires for us in the here and now, as well. This abundant life, however, is not about possessing fame and fortune and being preserved from any kind of heartache or struggle. What it does mean is that while Satan comes to steal, kill, and destroy our vision, joy, and purpose for life, Jesus came that we might have these things in abundance and find their foundation in Him. Let's face it—Jesus does not approve of this down-and-out, martyr mentality that is being carried around by far too many moms in our day. He desires that we thrive in the high calling of motherhood which He has so graciously bestowed upon us. We will only live in that abundant joy and purpose, however, if we first realize that our lives are not passing us by in this season of motherhood.

Far from it! In fact, right where we are in this season of mothering—no matter how challenging or difficult it may be—is precisely the life we have been called to by God. If we are being faithful to raise our children well, our lives couldn't possibly be passing us by, for we are living out our God-given mission right here in this very moment.

A Word to the Mama Who Wants "More"

What about the mamas out there who desire even more out of life? Perhaps they have personal dreams, goals, and ambitions beyond the sphere of motherhood. What does the gospel say to them in this situation?

First of all, as we have already seen, we are not called to find our ultimate fulfillment in motherhood. We are to find it first in Christ, and sometimes that includes living out specific gifts and talents He has given to us. As long as we are diligently insuring that we are not neglecting our families or failing to intentionally steward well the responsibility of motherhood, then there is much freedom beyond that for moms who have God-given gifts they feel called by Him to pursue.

Second, as we will see a few lies from now when addressing the myth that we "don't have time", moms have more time and opportunity on their hands to pursue creative endeavors, business ideas, ministry opportunities, etc. than they oftentimes realize. If God has called you to certain endeavors in addition to parenting, you have permission to pursue those. In fact, if it is a true calling on your life, you are expected to pursue it. It doesn't have to "pass you by".

For those business or ministry endeavors which truly are not for this season because they would take too much time away from your family, you have to believe that there will be a time for all that. If the Lord has called you to it, He will get you there when the time is right. We can surrender and safely entrust those future callings into the hands of our all-wise, all-loving God.

I know a lot of moms worry that if they stay at home with their children for years on end, they will have an outdated and unimpressive resume when they decide to go back to work at some point. Their fear is that they will not have been keeping up with the latest and greatest advancements in their field and will be ill-prepared (and perhaps not even hirable) when they do seek to enter the workforce again.

The answer to all of these fears (which do not come from God, see 2 Timothy 1:7) is faith and trust in an omnipotent, omniscient, omnipresent Creator who has promised to take care of you, provide for you, and work all things together for your good (Romans 8:28). We have to trust in a sovereign God who has our best interests at heart.

So, mama, the next time you are tempted to believe the lie that your life is passing you by, I want you to remember three things:

First, remember that your life could not possibly be "passing you by" because this life of a mother is specifically the life to which you have been called. It is an impactful, vastly important life that can alter the very course of nations.

Second, remember that there is time and opportunity, even in motherhood, to cultivate your gifts and pursue your various interests. For example, Sally Clarkson always encourages moms to do a lot of reading. Not only will this inspire our children to become readers themselves, but reading builds the intellect. And Sally saw value in being the most interesting person her kids knew. After all, as a homeschooling mom, she was their teacher and wanted to teach from an inspiring, interesting place. So, pursue your interests and hobbies—doing so could benefit your family!

Third, remember that "to everything there is a season, a time for every purpose under heaven" (Ecclesiastes 3:1). Do you not have the time to really pursue your business in this busy season of mothering littles? Do you not have the opportunity right now to serve in your community quite as much as you would like? That's OK! Our God is a sovereign God and knows when the best time would be for you to launch your business. He knows the time when your ministry endeavors will be needed the most. He knows at what future time your other pursuits could have the most impact.

Rest in the fact that He sees the big picture and knows what is best. Then live your life knowing that you are doing just that—living your life. It isn't passing you by as long as you are doing what God has called you to do. Embrace that, mama, making the very most of the beautiful life God has given you.

Motherhood Is a Woman's Highest Calling *Mothering Is Unimportant Work* My Identity Is to Be Found in Being a Mother *I Am to Find My Ultimate Fulfillment in Motherhood* Mommy Guilt Is Just Something I Have to Live With *It's Wrong for Me to Go to God Again and Again After I Fail* Theology Isn't for Moms *I Have to Be a Perfect Mom* I Have to Do it All *I Am Enough* My Children Would Be Better Off Having a Different Mom *I'm a Bad Mom* I'm Selfish If I Have Any "Me Time" *I Need a Lot of "Me Time"* Motherhood Has to Be Hard (And Hard Is Bad!) *I Have to "Keep My Act Together"* I Can't Have a Clean House While Raising Children *My Life Is Passing Me By* *I Am Responsible for My Child's Happiness* I Can't Do This Whole "Mothering Thing" *My Success as a Mom Is Directly Tied to How My Children Turn Out* I Don't Know What It Means to Be a Mom If I Only Have One Child *I Don't Have Time* My Postpartum Body Has to Look a Certain Way *Children Are a Nuisance and an Interruption* Children Are Really Expensive *Children Ruin a Marriage* My Focus Should Be on Rules and Regulations *The "Experts" Know Better How to Raise and Educate My Child Than I Do* The Most Important Thing Is My Child's Education *Good Moms Do "XYZ"* You Have to "Do" Motherhood the Way the Culture Tells You

LIE #19

I Am Responsible for My Child's Happiness

Do you ever find yourself thinking that you are the Holy Spirit? Oh, maybe you wouldn't say as much in so many words, but perhaps you have at least acted as if you have the power to produce change. I know I have! I sometimes think that if I just nag enough or inspire enough or say the perfect thing often enough, then I can get others to change in the way I think they should. I believe I can automatically make them happy, help them to see things from a more positive outlook, or get them to see things the way I do and adopt my point of view.

For whatever reason, many of us moms have adopted the idea that we are responsible for the happiness of our children. Alice submitted a comment via social media saying that this is precisely the lie she finds herself believing, which served as the inspiration for the title of this lie (so, thank you, Alice!).

In a lot of ways, it is understandable that we would easily fall prey to this lie—we want our children to be happy, we don't want them to experience heartache, and we realize that we are responsible for faithfully stewarding their little hearts and minds. As mothers, we have been given many responsibilities by God when it comes to parenting. We are to train up our children in the way they should go (Proverbs 22:6); speak to them of the ways of God, making every aspect of life a teaching moment for

God's truth (Deuteronomy 6:6-7); love our children (Titus 2:4); and raise them up in the nurture and admonition of the Lord, being careful not to provoke them to wrath (Ephesians 6:4). We are not, however, given the responsibility of ensuring their happiness.

There is a difference between being careful not to provoke your children to wrath and working like a crazy person to make sure your children are always happy. As we have already seen, happiness is circumstantial and, as such, differs from joy in that it is not something that can or will be experienced at all times. As adults, we understand this to be true. Then we become moms, and suddenly that all goes out the window. We love our little babies so much and feel the full weight of our responsibility to care for them well that we start believing we are responsible to ensure their happiness. We find ourselves believing that if they are not happy, it must be proof that we are doing something wrong.

I think this misconception is precisely why we see an onslaught today of entitled, selfish, bratty children. Parents have begun to believe that they are held responsible for whether or not their children are happy—so much so that when the moment arises and their child is suddenly unhappy, they instantly try to quickly fill the void and restore that coveted happiness. We see this all the time—from parents trying to bring happiness by buying their children more and more material goods, to parents giving in to their child's every wish in an effort to always keep them happy. This never ends well, and it ultimately never results in lasting happiness, either. What it does result in is selfish children who lose the ability to find joy in the little things of life (and happiness in the bigger things, as well, because nothing is ever enough for them). The irony is that when we work so hard as parents to always keep our kids happy, the end result is that no one is happy.

What we fail to remember is that our kids will experience a lack of happiness at one time or another, regardless of what kind of parents we are.

This is simply a result of the fall and cannot be avoided. When sin entered this world, so did guilt, shame, selfishness, hatred, anger, covetousness, pride, depression, disease, and loss. The sin nature is what is to blame for our lack of happiness, and the remedy is not found in children having perfect parents. The remedy is found in children being pointed to the perfect Savior who will do a sanctifying work in their hearts.

In life, we are responsible for stewarding well the people and possessions God has placed into our care. What we are not responsible for is the end result of that stewardship. That is all up to God. Paul wrote about this truth in 1 Corinthians 3:

> Who then is Paul, and who is Apollos, but ministers through whom you believed, as the Lord gave to each one? I planted, Apollos watered, but God gave the increase. So then neither he who plants is anything, nor he who waters, but God who gives the increase (vs. 5-7).

As great a minister of the gospel as Paul was, he nevertheless fully understood that he was powerless to bring about the desired result of seeing people saved. He could only be responsible for doing his part of planting the seed of truth through proclaiming the gospel. What resulted from his planting was entirely up to God; when increase did come then, Paul knew to whom glory was due.

It is the same for us as moms. We can't make our children happy. What we can do is be warm and loving, patient and kind, helpful and present with them. That is our part to play. It is God's part, however, to work through our faithfulness as moms and take what we do to produce in our children what we never could. As for our children and their happiness, they have a part to play, as well. They are responsible for their own attitudes and actions and can choose whether or not to be happy in any given moment. We can seek to train them in the self-control required to reject a complaining spirit and instead embrace a joyful one, but we are still not responsible for whether or not they choose to do so. That is between them and God.

So, rest, dear mama. Have you been given an important part to play in this grand work of child-rearing? Absolutely! Don't doubt that for a moment. But don't make the mistake of attempting to take on God's part, as well. As we have already touched on, anytime we attempt to take on the attributes of God which are characteristic of God alone, we wear ourselves out carrying burdens of responsibility the Lord never intended for us. Lay down the burdens. Lay down the weighty responsibility of your child's happiness. Do yourself and your children a favor and allow God to do His job while you do yours.

Satan wants your eyes focused on those responsibilities which are not yours so that he can distract you from fulfilling the responsibilities which actually are. Don't allow him to succeed. Instead, surrender your child's happiness into the Father's able hands, and watch an amazing thing happen—you and your children will begin to experience a new freedom and joy you have never had before. How do I know? Because our Lord is just gracious like that!

LIE #20

I Can't Do This Whole "Mothering Thing"

There is nothing quite like experiencing an exhausting day and being so completely ready for bed, only to have your baby decide that that very night is the perfect one for staying awake and rejecting the notion of "bed time". Through nights like these, I have come to the realization that I do not need to listen to a single thing I think or say when suffering from sleep deprivation. I have also come to understand that how frustrated and irrational I get when I'm feeling desperate for sleep is not completely representative of what kind of mom I am. Can I get an amen?

It has been on challenging nights like that when I have uttered the words of this lie: "I can't do this whole mothering thing. It's just too hard. There's no way I can do it anymore." It is in those awful moments of feeling completely drained and unable to put one foot in front of the other that the truth of God's Word comes to mind, reminding me that I can, in fact, mother my children. I can face another day. I can do what He's called me to do with the strength He provides. But there is even more good news beyond that!

Thoroughly Equipped and Prepared

When it comes to being able to believe that we truly can face another day in our mothering journeys (no matter what challenge or difficulty that day may bring), it all comes down to this: do we believe motherhood to be a good work? It truly does all boil down to our answer to this question. Because if we do believe it to be a good work, if we believe what we learned when discussing lie #2 about the importance and value of motherhood, then we can take great comfort in the following verses and what they mean for our days as mothers:

> All Scripture is given by inspiration of God, and is profitable for doctrine, for reproof, for correction, for instruction in righteousness, that the man of God may be complete, thoroughly equipped for every good work.
>
> —2 Timothy 3:16-17

> For we are His workmanship, created in Christ Jesus for good works, which God prepared beforehand that we should walk in them.
>
> —Ephesians 2:10

Do you believe that the work of motherhood—the work of providing nourishment, love, knowledge, care, warmth, shelter, and other provisions for your children—is a good work? If so, then on those incredibly hard days, you can remember that it is precisely when you are feeling weak that the power of Christ is resting upon you (2 Corinthians 12:9) and that you can do all things through His strength (Philippians 4:13). But you can take it a step further!

If you believe motherhood to be a good work, then you can rest in the fact that through the Word of God—that instruction manual we talked about a while back—you are already thoroughly equipped for that good work. That is a promise you can cling to when the going gets tough. Motherhood is challenging, and there are days we feel as if we simply cannot go on. But it is specifically on those days when we can cling to the truth that we have already been thoroughly equipped for the work of mothering. Not "partially equipped", or "a little equipped", or "almost equipped enough, but you have to come up with the rest of it on your own". No. Complete and thoroughly equipped. That's describing you, mama! That is your standing in your motherhood through the Word of God.

Beyond that (as if that weren't encouraging enough to know), if motherhood is a good work (and it certainly is), then the Lord prepared this work of mothering for us from the very beginning of time according to Ephesians 2:10. Before we were even born, before the Lord had ever formed us in the womb, before our own moms were even born, the Lord had planned for us to be His special workmanship. He planned for us to be created in Christ Jesus for the purpose of doing good works—good works which were prepared beforehand, before even one came to be. This means, then, that before we even became moms, the Lord had already prepared us for this role. He prepared us for the good—and hard—work of mothering. He designed this part of our lives to be an important aspect of the good work we would do for His Kingdom. Before the dawn of time, we were prepared for our good work of mothering, and the good work of mothering was prepared for us. Our God is not a deistic god, who created everything and then left us to our own devices, hoping we wouldn't screw it all up. Far from it! Our God is an intimately involved Father, a God who has called us to the life-changing work of mothering eternal souls and then thoroughly prepared and completely equipped us for that good work.

The next time you feel, as I have, that you just can't do this work of mothering, remember that it is a good work. Remember that God is faithful and stands by the truth of His Word. Remember that because the work of a mother is a good work, you can rest in the fact that He has promised to have already thoroughly equipped you for it. You can trust that He has already provided you with everything you need, having prepared you ahead of time for the work set before you on this day and every day. Have hope, mama! You can do this! He's got you covered.

LIE #21

My Success as a Mom is Directly Tied to How My Children Turn Out

Apparently, Satan has been working overtime in this particular area. When I reached out to ladies on social media, asking them to share with me what the biggest lies are that they have been believing about motherhood, an overwhelming majority of the responses I received were all along the same lines. Many women are believing that their success as moms is based upon how their children turn out:

> [I have believed that] if I am perfect, my kids (and marriage) will be perfect.
>
> —Molly

> [I have believed] that I've done something wrong (and I need to do better) if my kids make bad choices or aren't "perfect".
>
> —Julia

[I believed] that I was a good mom only if my adult children are doing well and following God.

—Kathy

I think one that I used to believe until I had a teenager is that kids are products of us, and if we do everything right in their upbringing they will automatically choose the right path. They are born people and have their own free will. Yes, we can and should teach them and guide them, but we can't force them. They need to come to the right decisions on their own. And sometimes after we've taught all we can, we just need to have the faith to let go and hand the reins over to the Lord who can touch their hearts and guide them better than we ever can.

—Brittany

[I've believed] that I am messing up my child.

—Angela

[I've believed] that our identity is in the success/ appearance/salvation of our children.

—Suzanne

> [I believe] that I'm a bad mom. When my kids make mistakes, this is the first place my mind goes.
>
> —Natalie

Perhaps you can relate to the struggles these women have faced in their mothering. I imagine you—or someone you know—have felt this way before because it can be easy to take the truth of mothering (that we are responsible to train up our children well) and turn it into a lie (that we are responsible for the outcome). As you can see, the truth which combats this lie is very similar to the truth that combats the one a few lies back about being responsible for our children's happiness: ultimately, the end results are not up to us.

Our Part—Being Faithful

We all know that we cannot make another person say, think, or do the things we want. We know we can't force another adult into being the kind of person we think they should be. Yet that is precisely what we end up doing with our children. We somehow think that what is true for adults simply can't be for our children. We believe that if we only use the right training method, discipline consistently and in the manner which best suits each particular child, read the Bible and pray with them daily, follow all the rules pertaining to baby care, tend to toddler tantrums the way in which the books tell us, implement the perfect homeschool curriculum, give our children the best devotional books available, always take them to church, and surround them with good, Christian friends, then all will be well. And if it isn't, then clearly there was some box left unchecked, some book that was not read, or some chore chart that was not implemented, and it is all our fault.

This, however, is not God's point of view. This kind of mindset actually takes God out of the equation entirely. Oh, He's factored in somewhere in the sense that we are placing value on taking our children to church, surrounding them with good company, and encouraging them to read a daily devotional. However, He is left out of the equation in the sense that we are acting as if we don't truly need Him. As long as we dot all our "i's" and cross all our "t's", we have it all covered, are guaranteed to produce perfect little Christians, and don't really need God's involvement, thank you very much. In a viewpoint such as this, there is no parenting by faith, there is no seeking God for help and wisdom, there is no praying for the Lord to touch the hearts of our children. There is simply a trusting in our own efforts. There is simply a belief that if I am a good mom, my kids will be good. If my kids are bad, then that must mean I am a bad mom. Our children are not little robots able to be controlled like this, however! Though we do carry powerful influence, we are powerless to absolutely ensure what kind of adults our children will become. Therefore, our success or failure in mothering is ultimately not based upon how our children turn out.

I know a few different homeschooling families who seemingly did everything right: they trained their children up in the nurture and admonition of the Lord, they raised their children with good standards, they were faithful church attendants. However, in each of these families, at least one of the children has grown up either to walk away from the faith, be unfaithful to their spouse, or else adopt the pro-abortion, pro-homosexuality liberal worldview. As much as it is heartbreaking to realize this as a mom, there simply are no guarantees. We can say all the right things, do all the right things, use all the right books, memorize all the right verses, and our children can still turn their backs on everything we ever taught them. What we have to understand then is that those choices our children make as adults are on them. They are not on us. We are simply called to be faithful to our responsibility to steward well the hearts of our children, consistently pointing them to the Lord. We are not, however, held responsible for the outcome. If you are training your children up in the way that they should go, you are a good mom. No choice they make later in life can change that.

The simple truth is that we need to stop listening to the age-old lie from Satan, which began in the Garden of Eden, that we can be like God. We are not sovereign. We cannot determine the course of human history or turn the hearts of our children in the direction we would like them to go. We are not omnipotent. This is as it should be. This is a good thing. And yet we try to heap the burden of omnipotence onto our shoulders, burdening ourselves with the belief that if our children ever make mistakes, then it's all on us; we must have made a blunder somewhere along the way. We need to let go of the lie that everything depends on us and rest in the freedom that comes with knowing that we are not held responsible for the outcome. We are only held responsible for the training. That's it. We are to plant the seed. Whether or not it grows is not our responsibility, nor does the end result make us a good or bad gardener.

God's Part—The Results

Do you remember the passage we read a few pages back which talked of the Lord being the One who causes our efforts to grow and produce results? I think it bears repeating here:

> Who then is Paul, and who is Apollos, but ministers through whom you believed, as the Lord gave to each one? I planted, Apollos watered, but God gave the

> increase. So then neither he who plants is anything, nor he who waters, but God who gives the increase.
>
> —1 Corinthians 3:5-7

As you can see, the responsibility of the results of our parenting efforts lies solely on the Lord. We cannot, therefore, believe ourselves to be "bad moms" if our children go astray. We cannot believe the lie that our success as moms is dependent upon how our children turn out. God is sovereign. The Bible also teaches, however, that man is responsible for his own choices (not the choices of others!). The results are then between your children and God—not you. I don't know about you, but I'm so grateful that we can rest in the Lord and His work in the hearts of our children. While we do have the responsibility to raise them in the nurture and admonition of the Lord and to train them in the way that they should go, our responsibility stops there. While we as parents should seek to fulfill the responsibilities we have been given, at the end of the day we have to rest in the Lord and His work. We plant the seed, but it is up to the Lord to give the increase.

That's actually quite a gift! It means that I don't have to endlessly strive after the desired result, keeping myself up at all hours of the night mentally toiling over the question of how exactly I am going to be sure to produce perfect children. I can cease my striving. I can rest from my toiling. I can do the job God has given me to do and relinquish control to Him, giving Him space to do the job He has to do. Rejoice in the fact that you are not the Holy Spirit, mama, and lay that burden down once and for all.

LIE #22

I Don't Know What It Means to Be a Mom If I Only Have One Child

When I asked for ladies on social media to share with me the lies they have been believing about motherhood, I didn't expect the following one to be submitted:

> If you have an only child you really don't know what it means to be a mom (Yes, people have said that to me).
>
> —Sheila

Reading this broke my heart for this sweet mama! As I stated, I did not expect to receive a lie like this one. Once I took some time to think about it, however, I didn't find it to be all that shocking that people have said this awful thing to Sheila.

You see, in Christendom today, there is something known as the "quiverfull" movement. You have likely heard of it. Though there are many different tenets held to in this movement, we will not go into all of them as they are beyond the scope of this book. However, the primary tenet, the one regarding children being blessings and something to be sought, is applicable here. This belief is certainly based on Scripture (see Psalm

127:3-5)—children are indeed a great blessing and a God-given reward. Because this is the case, we should never harbor disdain for children in our hearts. However, what may have been intended as a good thing—proclaiming the value of children—has inadvertently gone on to produce some less than stellar results.

What is happening far too often now is that, as a result of what is sometimes an overemphasis on the nature of children as blessings, you are looked down upon by those who have multiple children if you only have one. I realize that this does not occur across the board. I know quite a few simply amazing large families who would never dream of entertaining this kind of attitude; however, the point still remains. It is sometimes assumed that if you do not have additional children, then you have something against having more and perhaps do not understand the teachings of Psalm 127.

In all this emphasis of children being blessings as described in Psalm 127:3-5 (which in our pro-abortion culture is definitely an important topic to talk about at times), we have forgotten the truth of Psalm 127:1-2. That truth is that the Lord is the one who builds the house, not us. We see repeatedly in the Scriptures that God is the one who opens and closes the womb (see Genesis 2:21; Genesis 30:2, 22; 1 Samuel 1:19-20). He is the one ultimately in charge of fertility, not us. You can read all the right books, eat all the right foods, exercise all the right ways, balance your hormones with the right supplements, be intimate with your husband at the right time, desire a baby with all your heart, and still not have another baby. This is what large families in movements like the quiverfull one need to understand. They will readily admit that their children are gifts from God as a result of Him opening the womb, yet they sometimes forget that the opposite is also true. In the case of a woman with only one child, it may not be because she doesn't view children as blessings. It may be because God has, in this season, closed her womb. It could be that that family's particular quiver is full with one child. Having a "quiver full of children" (see Psalm 127:5) does not mean every family is to have ten children. It means every family is to be open to having their quiver filled with however many children with which the Lord sees fit to bless them—even if that is just one.

The truth that we have to remember and then embrace is that we each have our own unique "God-given puzzle" to live out, as Sally Clarkson would say. What this means is that we all have our own struggles, ups and downs, family dynamics, callings, victories, challenges, wisdom and knowledge acquired, etc., whether we have one child or twenty-one. The mama with one child should not be made to feel as if she doesn't understand motherhood because she doesn't have multiple little ones. If she is a mother, she knows what motherhood is like. She knows the struggles, hardships, heartaches, joys, and blessings of motherhood. How? Simply because she is a mother.

Here's another point to consider: everyone has their own version of hard. I've heard it said that everyone is maxed out right where they are. Meaning, a mom of one child may not be able to imagine having twins and therefore think herself incapable of ever handling multiples. A mom of two may feel maxed out and not be able to imagine ever feeling capable of adding a third baby to the mix. A mom of three may break out in a cold sweat at the thought of having four kids. I believe this is exactly as God designed us; He has designed us in such a way that we feel as if we are at full capacity in the very season in which we find ourselves. Why? So that we would rely on Him, trusting in His good will and sufficient provision. So that we would experience the beautiful truth of Deuteronomy 33:25 where we read, "as your days, so shall your strength be."

We imagine ourselves incapable of adding more children to the mix precisely because we have not yet been given the strength required for that. We are only given the strength to face what happens in this day we are living right now, with the Lord sovereignly adjusting that level of strength to perfectly go along with the events of each day. If you, like Sheila, have been treated as if you don't truly know what it's like to be a mom because you haven't dealt with the challenges that come with having multiple children, remember this: that mom of multiples wouldn't be able to handle having a large family, either, apart from the grace and strength of God that is made perfect in her weakness and measured out to her in the precise amounts required.

The fact of the matter is this: if you are a mama at all, whether you have one child or several, whether you have had your child(ren) biologically or through the gift of adoption, you know what it means to be a mom. You know exactly what it's like to be a mom simply because you are one—even if your motherhood doesn't quite look like the motherhood of the woman living next door.

Do not allow Satan a word in edgewise, making you feel as if you have not yet "arrived" because you only have one child. To use the southern vernacular, that's hogwash! If you are reading this and you are a mama of one child, hugs to you! I'm so sorry if you have ever felt that other moms didn't understand you or have viewed you as being unaware of what it really means to be a mom. Please know that your understanding of motherhood is not based on the number of children you have, but on the fact that you do have a child. Embrace the season you are in with that sweet child of yours and continue to be the awesome mama that you are!

LIE #23

I Don't Have Time

If you were to ask me what I would say is one of the biggest misconceptions that modern moms are buying into, I believe the answer is that they "don't have time". They think they need more than the twenty-four hours they have been given each day and are simply too busy for their husbands, for creative pursuits or projects, for pursuing friendships, or for Bible study and prayer in this busy season of motherhood. Talk about a clever lie of Satan! Did you catch the important people and pursuits in that list of things we're "too busy" for? What a trap we have fallen into in our day!

If you are that ultra-busy mom, stressed out and believing you don't have enough time, I would ask you this: are you busy doing what you want to do and what our culture expects of you, or are you busy doing what God has actually asked you to do? Oftentimes, there's a big difference. The fact of the matter is that many of those pursuits on the list of things we are too busy for are the very things for which God gave us time. We simply aren't using our time for those endeavors, instead choosing to dedicate our time to Netflix, social media, too many work projects, and other pursuits which are, at the end of the day, not nearly as important as those things we are letting fall by the wayside in the process.

If I believe that God is sovereign and not in the business of making mistakes, then I have to believe it was a good thing for Him to put precisely twenty-four hours into each day. The time we have been given is just as it should be. I do have time. If I am feeling overwhelmed and filled-to-the-max with list upon list of things to do, then the logical conclusion is either that I have added too many expectations and tasks to each day, or else I am wasting a lot of my time on those things which are ultimately not important. We need to, as my friend Naomi has said, "not pray for God to help us juggle all these balls we have in the air, but ask Him if there are any we are supposed to stop juggling."

Mamas, I want us to take back the time we have been graciously given by God, stewarding it well and redeeming it, "for the days are evil" (Ephesians 5:16). When all is said and done, we will give an account for what we did with the time He entrusted to us. Will we have to say we squandered it away scrolling through social media, or will we be able to say we were discerning of those things which were of lasting importance, intentionally putting our time to the pursuit of them?

Too Busy for God

What is usually the first thing to go when the busyness invades? Typically, it is our time with the Lord. What a grievous mistake we make here. We truly are shooting ourselves in the foot, depriving ourselves of the source of the strength and vision required for faithful, God-centered mothering. How often do we as women feel downright weak in our marriages and in our mothering? When we feel spiritually, emotionally, and mentally sluggish, when we find ourselves going through moments where we feel like utter failures, when we begin to allow Satan and his lies to invade our thinking, we can know that we have relegated God to the back burner for far too long.

Mamas, we are sucking the very lifeblood out of our marriages and our mothering when we move Bible study and prayer to the very bottom of our to-do list.[19] We are taking the most important practice—that of meeting with God—that would make all the difference in the world for ourselves and our families and treating it as if it is not important. In reality, as we have already seen, being in the Word is where our strength comes from for our lives. It follows then that we would be weakening our endurance and abilities in these areas when we are not in communion with God on a regular basis. Just as we would not go without physical food to energize and nourish our bodies, likewise we should not be going without spiritual food, the Word of God, to energize and nourish our souls.

> But He [Jesus] answered and said, "It is written, 'Man shall not live by bread alone, but by every word that proceeds from the mouth of God.'"
>
> —Matthew 4:4

> Jesus said to them, "My food is to do the will of Him who sent Me, and to finish His work."
>
> —John 4:34

> For the word of God is living and powerful, and sharper than any two-edged sword, piercing even to the division of soul and spirit, and of joints and marrow, and is a discerner of the thoughts and intents of the heart.
>
> —Hebrews 4:12

> All Scripture is given by inspiration of God, and is profitable for doctrine, for reproof, for correction, for

> instruction in righteousness, that the man of God may be complete, thoroughly equipped for every good work.
>
> —2 Timothy 3:16-17

We are muddling our understanding of what are true, right priorities when we are not regularly taking in the wisdom of God's Word and His perspective for life. We are depriving ourselves of the comfort, knowledge, insight, encouragement, strength, and help required in order to live this one life well. We are going through life without the instruction manual. Too often we, in an effort to be nice and understanding, will tell moms with young children that we know how busy they are and how impossible it is to spend time in the Word in this season, giving them a free pass for ignoring God's Word. That's not a very nice thing to say, however, as it deprives that mom of what she actually needs. It likewise is simply not true to the Biblical text or to God's priorities for His people—moms or otherwise. The Lord gave us the great gift of His Word precisely because He expects us to be in it and benefit from it, viewing it as our roadmap for life.

The problem is that we have entertained the mistaken idea that unless our quiet time situation is "perfect" (that we are up before our kids, have a hot cup of coffee nearby, are sitting in our favorite comfy chair with candle lit, music playing, journal and Bible in hand, and a free hour in which to study and pray), then it's all for naught and there's no point in it. If our only option is to read for just five quick minutes before the baby wakes up, or if we only get to do our reading once the kids are all already awake around us, we believe all is lost. This mistaken idea is evidence of our placing more faith and power in the circumstances surrounding our Bible reading than in the actual Bible itself and the God behind it. Do we actually believe the Word to be alive and active or not? Do we really believe it will not "return void" (Isaiah 55:11), or do we think God lied in this verse? Our answers to these questions (after we have searched our hearts in this area) will determine our attitude and our outlook when our desire for a quiet "quiet time" goes unmet. The power of God's Word is not dependent upon how long we read it or if we have a hot cup of coffee and no children nearby. The power of God's Word is in the very fact that it is God's Word and that it "shall not return to Me void, but it shall accomplish what I please, and it shall prosper in the thing for which I sent it" (Isaiah 55:11). I propose that the "perfect quiet time" is simply any time you open the Word of God—no matter what the extenuating circumstances.

The sobering reality is this: we cannot expect our children to believe us when we say God's Word is important if they never see us reading it or actually acting as if it's important. It may be cliché, but that doesn't make it any less true—actions do speak louder than words. We need to be showing our kids that we are actually practicing what we preach, that we're not merely telling our children they should be in the Word, but that we are actually in the Word ourselves.

Stick with me here a moment, and please do not despair, mama! If you are a busy wife and mama and feel as if you just do not have time to spend with the Lord, I'm going to debunk that myth for you with some practical tips for how you can easily incorporate God's Word into your own everyday life. The truth is that you do have real opportunities to make daily time with the Lord a reality right away, even in the midst of your busy life. Incorporating spiritual disciplines into your daily walk really isn't as hopeless a concept as you might think! Not all of the ideas I'll share with you here will necessarily work well in your particular season of life, but I imagine you'll find something that will.[20]

How to Spend Time in the Word as a Busy Wife and Mama

- Get up a little earlier than your kiddos in order to spend time with the Lord. For me, having that time first thing in the morning makes a big difference for the rest of my day.
- Are you a nursing mama? Having to sit down and nurse is the perfect pause button in your day for you to get in some Bible or prayer time!
- Are you frequently up in the middle of the night with your child? Use this time to commune with the Father.
- Download a Bible app onto your phone. This way, you will literally be taking God's Word with you wherever you go! Read it while sitting in a waiting room; turn on the audio option and be read to while you are driving, while you are taking a shower, cooking dinner, or folding laundry. The possibilities are endless. The YouVersion app is a great option to consider.
- Have your quiet time while your little ones are napping.
- Keep your Bible in the bathroom. I know it sounds crazy, but if you intentionally add a little reading into every opportunity you get, you'll get a lot more reading in than you think! For example, read while brushing your teeth! I do this all the time.
- Do you have time to be on social media? Then you have ample time to read the Word or be in prayer. You just have to want time with the Father more than you want time on social media.

Pray about that—the Lord will work in your heart to cause you to want to know and seek Him more.

- Keep your Bible open on your kitchen counter so you can read quick verses here and there as you go throughout your day.

- Post verses in your car and throughout your home: on a little decorative chalk board in the living room, on an index card on your bathroom mirror, etc.

- Read the Bible out loud to your children and discuss it. Lead them in prayer time every day. Instead of thinking we always have to be in our Bibles only when we are by ourselves and everything is quiet, we can kill two birds with one stone and have our daily Bible reading time coincide with our endeavor to teach God's Word to our children.

- Have Bible-based worship music playing in your home and car. Seeds Family Worship, Psalms set to music, and songs by Keith and Kristyn Getty are all great for this.

You see, we busy wives and mamas truly do have ample opportunity to meet with our Father and receive the wisdom, strength, and encouragement we need to live our lives well. We just have to be intentional in the way in which we use those opportunities.

Far from being just a nice idea I want to point you towards, I find that, this practice of a daily "quiet time" is positively critical to the entire rest of my day and how it goes. When I start out my day with the Lord, I tend to be far happier, more patient with my children, less stressed when things get busy, and more in the present moment. I am better at discerning between proper priorities for my day and less-important pursuits. The story is far different, however, when I miss my time with the Lord! My guess is, the same would hold true for you, as well.

Too Busy for Our Husbands

We moms have a terrible tendency to place our children and their needs above our husbands and the continued cultivation of our marriages. Is it any wonder the divorce rate is the same in the church as in the world at large, with many marriages ending after twenty or more years? Too many marriages are breaking up today as a direct result of husband and wife forgetting each other in the busyness of parenting, and finding that they no longer know one another when the nest is empty and they finally take the time to actually look at each other again.

We know we should focus on our marriages in the midst of busy seasons of parenting, but the question becomes how, practically speaking, do we put our husbands first in the midst of daily demands, duties, and deadlines? What is the mantra of "put your husband first" (second only to God, of course!) supposed to look like when you, as a wife and mama, are in the thick of dirty diapers, temper tantrums, loads of laundry, cooking duties, cleaning schedules, and more?

As with Bible study, I believe we actually have far more opportunities at our disposal for focusing on our husbands than we oftentimes think we do. Here are just a few practical tips which I hope will help to paint a picture for you of what this could look like in your own home. Perhaps something in this list will get you started thinking about how you can express, in a tangible, visible way, that your husband comes first on your list of importance and priorities.

Have Regular Date Nights

This is so important! Don't start throwing stones at me here in frustration, though, thinking this to be an impossibility in your current season of life. Stick with me here!

Our daughter was born on January 11, 2015, and two months later our first wedding anniversary was fast approaching. It was obvious my husband wanted to take me out to celebrate, and I definitely wanted to go! It would be our first date since our daughter was born and would be such a special occasion for us to celebrate. But as much as I wanted to go, "new mommy" thoughts kept running through my head: *Is this OK? Is it OK for me to leave my young daughter with someone else so that I can go out with my husband?*

It wasn't long before I realized that not only was there nothing wrong with going, but that going would actually be a very good thing for me to do! We left Anna with my parents for a couple hours while we went out to dinner and celebrated the first year of our marriage. That night, that special time to get away and celebrate our marriage, was such a blessing! We decided then and there that we needed to be intentional about dedicating time to having regular date nights. For us, that currently means that at least once a month, we leave Anna, James, and all their accoutrements with grandparents, an aunt and uncle, or a close family friend, and Owen and I go on a pre-planned date, enjoying every minute of the opportunity to focus solely on each other.

I cannot encourage you enough to do the same! Depending on what stage of marriage and parenting you are in, this may mean once a week, once a month, or once a quarter. Whatever it is for you, though, plan it, mark the calendar, and do what you have to do to make it happen! If you don't have family close by to babysit your little ones, perhaps "barter" with friends from church. Have them watch your kids so you can go out, and then watch their kids another day so they can go out. Whatever it is, be intentional and do it.

Another thing to keep in mind is that you can make date nights out of your time at home! Sometimes having a date night out just isn't feasible (such as when you have a newborn). That's OK! Be creative and make a date out of your evening at home together. Regularly make a habit of getting the kiddos to bed early so that you can have some much-needed couple time. Remember—your marriage is to come first, regardless of what stage of parenting you are in (this doesn't mean, of course, that you ignore the needs of your newborn in order to have an uninterrupted date night at home with your husband; it simply means that our focus should be on making our husbands still feel just as loved, needed, and important now as they did before the babies arrived). The important thing here is our heart—not exactly how often we have a date night.

Actively and intentionally keeping your marriage first will not only benefit you and your spouse. It will also provide a sure, secure environment for your children to grow up in and show them a picture of how God designed marriage to be. We as moms and dads are to be leading our children by example. They need to be able to look at us and know that when they grow up and get married, they can—and should!—always put their spouse and marriage first, as well.

Seek Your Husband's Preferences Regarding Your List of Priorities

Mamas have so much on their to-do lists. Can I get an amen? Everything from childcare to cooking to laundry to cleaning to grocery shopping tends to fall on our shoulders (though I must say here that I have an amazing husband who does step in and get things done when he can tell I need help; he's a blessing!). With all the tasks that can take up our time, energy, and attention on any given day, it can sometimes seem impossible to actually keep our husbands first. Here is one great tip in three easy steps for how you can do that in a practical way. This is actually something I implement with my own husband on a regular basis:

Make a list of all the things you have to do on any given day/week (e.g., laundry, cooking, childcare, etc.)

Show your husband the list and ask him to prioritize those things in order from most important to him to least important (e.g., Does he want a home-cooked meal each evening? Does he want you to be a couponer? Does he appreciate ironed shirts? Does he want you to be the one to do the dishes?)

Follow through on his list of priorities first!

Sometimes, depending on your stage of life, it can seem impossible to have the children playing quietly, dinner hot and ready, and the house all picked up when your husband walks in the door. If, however, instead of stressing out trying to get all this accomplished for his arrival home, you focused instead on which tasks mean the most to your husband and would bless him the most, you can relax a little and just focus on doing those things. Some husbands would love to find dinner ready the minute they walk in the door. Others could care less about that, but would rather the living room be relatively free of clutter upon their arrival home. Finding out what that special thing is for your own unique husband will free your time from those less important household tasks so that you can instead focus on what would truly bless him the most. In the end, doing this will also leave you with a little more free time and breathing room than you would otherwise have! This will be a double blessing to your husband, for it will show him that you care about his preferences and what will make your house a haven in his eyes, and will also leave you with more time to devote to other areas of your life.

Make His Homecoming at the End of Each Day Something Special

I don't know about you, but I can easily fall into the trap of shouting, "Hey, honey!" from across the room or down the hall when my husband gets home. How much better it would be for me to take just one quick second, stop what I'm doing, and greet my man at the door with open arms, a kiss, and the knowledge that I'm happy he's home! I realize that offering your husband this kind of greeting is not feasible every single day in each and every season of your life. These ideas are not about placing yokes of law and bondage on you, mama. Instead, they are about providing you with simple little ideas that you can implement as the situation allows. In all actuality this is a heart thing. Do we want to put our husbands first? If so, then we can put this and other ideas into practice as much as possible, understanding that even if we go days without accomplishing some of them, the overarching picture our husbands will receive from us will still be one of love and devotion to them. And that's the important thing.

Train Your Kids to Honor Their Daddy

Again, we lead by example. We train by example. Teach your children to honor their daddy by honoring him yourself through your words and actions. Gently, lovingly, and kindly make it clear to your children that the world does not revolve around them. For example, train them not to interrupt when you are talking to Daddy. This kind of thing will result in a home which does not first and foremost revolve around the kids and their desires. In the long run, this will greatly benefit your kiddos just as it does your husband and your marriage.

Learn All You Can About His Likes and Dislikes

What is your husband's favorite meal, favorite music, or favorite way to take his coffee? Do you know? If not, ask him! If so, make that meal for him when you can, have that music playing when he gets home, prepare his coffee that way. What are his least favorite foods? Don't make a habit of cooking them! Honor his preferences. I love water chestnuts, but the mere thought of them makes my husband sick. So, as much as I love them, I refrain from using them in my cooking. This is a simple little thing, but it can speak volumes to my husband of how much I love him. Make it a habit to study your husband and know how he feels about things.

Ask His Opinions; Don't Rush Ahead of Him

As women, we tend to have our own plans, things we want to do, places we want to go, etc. There is nothing wrong with that. We do, however, need to make it a habit to seek our husband's opinion and advice on these things and not race ahead of him. We need to remember that when we got married, we became one; we need to take into account our husband's own plans and desires, too!

Let Him Know He's on Your Mind

Let your husband know that even among the busyness that is your daily life, he is still on your mind. Send him flirty little texts or hide notes in his lunch bag. Don't let him doubt that he is important to you and that you love him and think about him often.

Brainstorm Ways to Be a Better Helper Even More Suitable to Your Own Unique Husband

We as wives were created to be helpmeets to our husbands (Genesis 2:18). That's one of the reasons why it is so sad to see women placing motherhood and their children ahead of marriage and their husbands. Motherhood is important and children are a great blessing. But I think sometimes we, especially in conservative circles, place the truth that children are a blessing so far in the forefront of our minds that we tend to forget that we were not first and foremost created to be mothers. That was not the primary purpose behind the Lord's creating women. No. First and foremost the reason God created us was in order that we might provide man with a partner, someone to come alongside him and aid him in the work we were both given to fill the earth and subdue it (Genesis 2:18, 1 Corinthians 11:9). We need to remember this. We also need to remember, though, that there is no one-size-fits-all method for how, specifically, to live out this role.

Certainly, there are helpful principles that each couple across the board can implement, but the exact way in which they apply them will look different, and that is OK! In fact, that's a good thing. The Lord created us all with different interests, talents, personalities, and family dynamics, and He wants us to live those out, displaying His creativity as we do so. The main thing is that we, as wives, place our husbands and our role as helper and partner first. How that looks in each individual marriage is going to be different, though, because the needs of each husband are different. I love how Genesis 2:18 is worded. Depending on the version you read, it may say, "a help meet for him" or a helper "suitable for him". Either way, we are being told that we were created to be the helper our particular husband needs us to be. We need to be "meet" for him or suitable for him uniquely. That's why it is important to study your own husband and learn what he does and does not need. Make it your mission to be a student of your husband and learn all you can about him as you go through your journey of marriage. This practice will reap many blessings for your whole family!

Did you notice how many of these ideas don't take much time at all to implement? Even the busiest moms can work to intentionally put their husbands first. It's a lie of Satan to think otherwise. At the end of the day, putting your husband first (and how exactly you will do so) is a heart thing. Where is your heart? Does it desire to put your husband first and make him feel like he is the most important person in your world? Then take that wonderful desire and apply it as best you can in your current season of life. You, your husband, and your children will be glad you did!

Too Busy for Creativity

Mama, do you remember the woman you were before you became a mom?[21] Maybe you were the woman who loved to write and had dreams of becoming an author. Perhaps you loved art and regularly set aside time to fashion a masterpiece on a canvas. Maybe you were a voracious reader. Maybe you felt so alive when you were out volunteering at your local soup kitchen or women's shelter. Perhaps you ran an Etsy shop. Or maybe it was something else entirely!

Whatever your interest was, though, it was there. You had hobbies. You had your own unique set of gifts that you knew were entrusted to you by God to use for His glory. Then you became a mom. Suddenly you bought into the lie that you are now too busy for any hobbies or talents or interests outside of those pertaining to your children.

Now, don't get me wrong—your children are to be your primary priority (after God and your husband), and your calling to mother them well and raise them up in the nurture and admonition of the Lord is a vastly important, world-changing mission that is not to be ignored. I am not at all saying you need to take big chunks of time, leave your kids with other people, and go out and find your "mission". You are living your primary mission when you are with your family, and we would certainly do well to remember that.

But that isn't all you're called to, mama. It isn't the only thing for which you have been given time. It isn't meant to be your sole mission 24/7/365 for the rest of your life.

I want to take a moment to give you permission and inspiration. Permission to go beyond merely the "me-time" concepts of going out for a manicure or taking the time to watch your favorite TV show, and to instead yearn for more. Inspiration to think back to when you weren't yet a mom, remember what your own unique interests and gifts were before the children came, and consider how you might be able to implement some of those again little by little in each and every season of life.

After all, Satan would like nothing more than for you to spend all of your time every single day solely on entertaining, caring for, and focusing on your children and their needs. Again, you do need to remember that, as a mother, one of your primary roles is to actually mother your children. However, Satan wants you to have a child-centric home which was something we were, in fact, never meant to have. The enemy wants your home to be a child-centric one because he knows that such a family culture tends to produce children who have little to no understanding of the concepts of authority and submission, sacrifice, humility, selflessness, gratitude, or working as a team.

In addition, Satan wants the whole of your time to be focused on your kiddos because he knows that is a surefire recipe for burnout and loss of vision in your life as a mom. When all of our time is focused on changing diapers, feeding toddlers, playing with the kids, doing their laundry, answering their questions, and more (all of which are indeed super important!), we quickly lose sight of the big picture, of the actual importance of what we are doing, and we can easily become despondent, discouraged, and sometimes even a little bitter.

My mothering hero, Sally Clarkson, so often says that a mom at home alone with her children all day every day can quickly become a target for Satan. That's so very true! Here's what I want you to do today, mama. Think back again to what your favorite hobbies and interests were, ponder how the Lord has uniquely gifted you, and then brainstorm ways you can incorporate into your daily life right now just a little bit of time for those pursuits.

Take it from me—at the time of this writing I am a stay-at-home mom of two kiddos two and under (and the homeschooling nanny of a third). Yet I have a blog, recently started a podcast, and am now working on this book. Not because I'm some superwoman. Please hear me on that! I'll repeat it if need be: *I am not superwoman*! Rather, I dedicate bits of time to these pursuits in the mornings before my kiddos get up, for a little bit some evenings while my husband is playing with our little ones, or on an occasional afternoon while my mom spends some time with our children. It doesn't have to be hard or complicated! You just have to draw up a plan that works well for you and your family. Additionally, you have to be willing to tweak it as need be as you go through the various changing seasons of your life as a mom.

The main thing is that you remember this: you can and should instill a little creativity into your everyday life, whatever that looks like for you. Be the woman God made you to be while exercising and putting to good use the gifts that He gave to *you*. Doing so, while exercising them within the confounds of proper priorities, is far from selfish or wrong. I believe it is obedience to the God who gave you those gifts and who expects you to use them in the first place, both in and out of the sphere of motherhood. Because here's the thing—when we are told in 1 Corinthians 12 that all members of the Body of Christ have been given spiritual gifts to use for the sake of the Church, mothers are not excluded. Now, granted, using those gifts specifically for the good of your family and in the context of teaching your children is a very important aspect of a mother using her God-given gifts. But, as long as you're not neglecting your family, your use of your gifts doesn't have to stop there, but can truly be dedicated to benefitting the Church as a whole.

Additionally, you have likely heard it said that you can't pour from an empty cup. If you want to pour your very best self into the important little people in your life, you are going to have to first fill *your* cup. You'll have to take the illustration from the movie *Mom's Night Out* and put it into practice: if you are on an airplane in an emergency which requires the use of oxygen, you need to put on your own oxygen mask before you tend to your seat mates and put on theirs. Because if you are without oxygen, the likelihood is that you will be unable to tend to the needs of the others on the plane with you.

Not only is using our gifts beneficial for ourselves and for the Church, but when we are taking the time, as our current season of motherhood allows, to pursue interests and to use our God-given talents, it benefits our children, as well. We are providing our children with a tangible example of how they themselves can, and should, do the same! If all our children ever see is us toiling over our to-do lists and living a life characterized by busyness, that is exactly what they will likely grow up to do themselves. What a waste of their gifts that would be!

Let's lead by example then, mamas. Let's encourage and inspire our children to use their God-given gifts for His Kingdom as we seek to do the same ourselves. And let's not deprive the church of the spiritual gifts God gave each of us to use for the benefit of that Kingdom (see 1 Corinthians 12).

Too Busy for Community

I've already shared the wisdom of Sally Clarkson when it comes to isolated motherhood, but it bears repeating here: When women are home alone with their children day in, day out, largely isolated from the outside world, they quickly become one of the biggest targets for Satan and his discouraging lies. One of these lies is the one Amber shared:

> That we can or should do it alone.

One of the saddest things I hear moms say is, "I'm just too busy in this season of life to have friends. With all these little kids, I just don't have time to cultivate friendships right now." Every time I hear a mom say that, I want to put my arm around her and answer, "Sweet sister, you are too busy *not* to have friends!"[22]

Throughout the Word, both in direct teaching as well as in story, we see the importance God placed upon friendships. Just think for a moment on the relationships between David and Jonathan or Ruth and Naomi or Paul and his various co-laborers in the truth. Satan understands the importance of community, so he wants to get you all alone, isolated from anyone who would dare attempt to encourage you in your faith, point you to the Lord, or inspire you to greatness in your mothering. The bottom line is Satan wants you thinking you are too busy to cultivate friendships in this season of your life.

After all, he knows that it is in this very season of being neck-deep in mothering when you need inspiring friendships the most! He also knows that if he can get you to make excuses now for not fostering friendships, he can get you so in the habit of doing this that you will continue to later in life, as well, so that no matter what season of life you are in, you will always think of yourself as being too busy for such things. Don't be deceived into making the early years of child-raising out to be a prison wherein you have no ability to fellowship with the outside world. That's a lie, plain and simple, and we need to stop believing it.

Three Reasons Christian Friendship is So Crucial

1. Christian friends are there to help us in times of need.

I love the passage in Ecclesiastes which says,

> Two are better than one, Because they have a good reward for their labor. For if they fall, one will lift up his companion. But woe to him who is alone when he falls, For he has no one to help him up. Again, if two lie down together, they will keep warm; But how can one be warm alone? Though one may be overpowered by another, two can withstand him. And a threefold cord is not quickly broken.
>
> —Eccelesiastes 7:9-12

Whether it's hard work that needs to be done, a fall into sin, a season of temptation, or another time of great need, friends are invaluable! We need each other. God made us that way! It's foolish then for us to believe ourselves to be too busy for such a crucial aspect of life as community. Don't think yourself wiser than God and try to go it alone. Find a good friend and you will go through life stronger, more encouraged, and more fruitful in your Christian walk and your work for the Kingdom.

2. Christian friends edify you and are used by God in your sanctification process.

Proverbs 27:17 says, "As iron sharpens iron, so a man sharpens the countenance of his friend." In his Bible commentary, Matthew Henry writes:

> This intimates both the pleasure and the advantage of conversation.... Wise and profitable discourse sharpens men's wits... It sharpens men's looks, and, by cheering the spirits, puts a briskness and liveliness into the countenance... Good men's graces are sharpened by converse with those that are good... Men are filed, made smooth, and bright, and fit for business (who were rough, and dull, and inactive), by conversation.[23]

True, godly friends are a fantastic resource for renewing your mind in the things of God, expanding your knowledge and understanding of the Christian worldview, and fine-tuning your thought process in regards to all areas of life. This is especially true for busy moms. When we are in the thick of mothering and feeling exhausted, overwhelmed, or downtrodden, a conversation with an encouraging, God-centered friend who will point us to Christ and renew our perspective is exactly what we need—not binge-watching Netflix, scrolling through social media, or going out for a shopping spree. Though those may help us feel better for a time, what we really need is to have our minds renewed with the lasting, refining, inspiring, encouraging truths of God's Word—the truths that we will have fed back to us by godly friends.

3. Christian friendship is a powerful tool for keeping your heart in close fellowship with the Lord and His ways.

We often hear that "bad company corrupts good character" (1 Corinthians 15:33). The opposite is also true—good company grows and encourages the development of good character. Christian friendship is an incredibly powerful influence for good in your heart and life. Esther Edwards Burr (1732-1758), daughter of Jonathan and Sarah Edwards and mother of the infamous Aaron Burr Jr., perhaps said it best when she wrote:

> I esteem religious conversation one of the best helps to keep up religion in the soul, excepting secret devotion, I don't know but the very best. Then what a lamentable thing 'tis to be so neglected by God's own children.[24] (And, I would add—what a lamentable thing to neglect God's own children!)

She went on to write:

> I look on the ties of friendship as sacred... A person who looks upon himself to be friendless must of all Cretures be missarable in this life – 'Tis the life of life.[25] (spelling her own)

I couldn't agree more. If you want to be armed for spiritual battle, grow in your Christian walk, and be encouraged and bolstered for the hard seasons of life, then you need friends. I said above that you are too busy not to have friends because you are just that—busy. You are so busy with all the cares of this life (e.g., the struggles of marriage, the questions of motherhood, the stresses of health issues, whatever it is) that you absolutely must have godly friends by your side to see you through.

Cultivating Friendship as a Busy Mom

Now for the practical side of things! You may be sitting there thinking, *Yeah, I see the importance of friendship now, but how do you expect me to dedicate time to it when I'm just so busy?* My answer would be this: if you are too busy to find time for friends, you are busy doing a lot of extra things God never asked you to do. How do I know that? Ask yourself this: if God places a huge importance on friendship, then don't you think He has made a way for you to pursue it, even in this season of your life? When we describe ourselves as being "too busy" for friendship, we are thinking ourselves to be wiser than God, better at prioritizing than He is, more understanding of what is and is not important. We are wrong. I know I've said it before, but I'll say it again: I love how my friend Naomi said in our recent podcast interview that we are asking the Lord the wrong question. We are always asking Him how we are supposed to handle all the different balls we are juggling when, in reality, we ought to be asking Him if we are busy juggling balls He never handed to us, but that we took on ourselves. And then, upon hearing His answer, be willing to lay them down.

It has been said so much that it has almost become cliché, but it's so true—we make time for the things that are important to us. If we are dedicated to aligning our lives with the Lord's priorities and those things He deems to be important, then we will embrace His view of the importance of friendship and make the time to pursue it. The hard part is that doing so will require a relinquishing of some of the other pursuits we hold most dear:

- Many of us are guilty of giving time to Netflix more often than to a friend we invite over for coffee.
- Many of us are exchanging face-to-face fellowship for social media friends that sometimes we barely even know.
- Many of us keep things surface-level with the online friends we do have when we could instead go a step further and really cultivate a true, deep camaraderie and friendship with them.

The fact of the matter is this: if we are too busy for friendship, I'm afraid we only have ourselves to blame. If women hundreds of years ago—who had no modern conveniences and instead had to grow, prepare, and preserve all their food, make all their own clothes, and wash everything by hand—still placed great importance on pursuing friendship and cultivating community, so can we, sweet sisters! It all comes down to whether or not we grasp the importance of it in the first place. With that in mind, here are some ideas to help you get started cultivating community:

- I don't like to use the quote "It takes a village" because of the one from whom it originated, but the basic concept is very true: it takes community, encouragement, and friendship to do this mama thing well! We need each other in order to be bolstered in our endeavors. So, how about scheduling a play date with your friend who has littles of her own? Have her over and enjoy coffee or tea together while your babies play, or meet up at the park!

- Take an hour or two one evening or on a Saturday, let your little ones have special Daddy time, and meet up with a friend for a nice, long chat.

- Text your friends uplifting Bible verses or lessons learned through your quiet time that day or leave them little messages of encouragement when they come to mind. This just takes a minute to do, and means so much! My sweet friend, Geneva, is a pro at this.

- Check in with a friend on a regular basis with just a short little note asking her how she's doing. Again, this doesn't take long! My friend, Amber, is awesome at this.

Those are just a few ideas to hopefully get you started and to inspire you to come up with your own ways you can be about the business of fostering friendship in your life.

The Bottom Line

Here is what we have to remember: The Lord would not commission us with the tasks of tending to our relationship with Him, our husbands, our children, our homes, our talents and gifts, and our friendships and ministries, and then leave us without the time to do so. He doesn't want us to lose ourselves in motherhood, forgetting the Christian, woman, wife, and friend we were created to be, while we instead focus solely on the role of "mom". He wants us to take time however we can (there are actually many tips and tricks at your disposal) to cultivate beauty and life, to pursue our passions, to enjoy tea time with friends, to listen to a favorite Pandora playlist, have a once-in-a-while manicure at the mall, go out on romantic date nights with our husbands, have fun putting to use the gifts He gave to us, take time to literally smell the roses or watch the sun set, and actually taste the myriad foods He created (but which we are usually in too big of a rush to delight in and notice). Enjoy life! Glorify God as you do so! Cultivate a life-giving atmosphere by being a woman who is full of life and the joy which comes through being a child of God! Remember that life is ultimately found at the feet of Jesus as Mary understood and Martha learned (Luke 10:38-42).

The time is there. It is yours, given to you by God. The question is: what are you going to do with it?

LIE #24

My Postpartum Body Has to Be a Certain Way

I'll never forget the way I felt about my new mama body immediately following the birth of my first baby. Those first few weeks postpartum were just plain hard as I wrestled to come to terms with how my belly, in particular, looked now. Forget the fact that my body had just been used by God to sustain life for nine months. Forget the fact that my body was what actually allowed a new human being to enter the world. Forget the fact that my muscles, skin, ligaments, and more had stretched to the limits in order to sustain the blessing of new life. It was that very stretching of skin and muscle that was the problem here! The resulting sagginess, stretch marks, and poochiness (that has now become a new word, mamas!) were precisely what I didn't like. I remember being so thankful that intimacy with my husband was off-limits for those first six weeks postpartum, because I was able to hide behind that need of my body to heal. I could hide behind the medical recommendation of no intimacy for six weeks and wouldn't have to have my husband see me in all my postpartum glory (or lack thereof, as I felt it was). It's sad to me now that I ever even felt that way (and it was sad to my sweet husband when I finally told him!), but I did. And I know you probably have, too. A lady on Facebook shared with me the following lie she has believed:

> [I've believed] that your body can (and should) bounce back once the baby is born.
>
> —Selina

While it is true that our bodies are absolutely amazing in their many God-given abilities to "bounce back" following all sorts of different life events, and while it is also true that the way your body looks immediately postpartum is not how it will still look even six months out, our bodies will nevertheless always bear the marks of pregnancy in one way or another. Our stretch marks may fade, some of our sagginess may tighten back up, and working out may produce some amazing results, but our bodies will never completely be the exact way they were before we became moms. And you know what I have come to believe? There is great beauty to be found in that fact!

I used to lament the fact that because I got pregnant with Anna a mere month into our marriage, my husband didn't get to experience my pre-baby body very long at all. There are still days when I am prone to want to hide certain parts of myself from my husband because I wish they were different. Our culture, with its air-brushed models and expectations of bodily perfection, doesn't help matters any. I want you to know, though, mama, what I have come to know: there is so much beauty in the postpartum nature of our bodies if we are willing to view them through gospel-colored glasses.

Our Bodies—A Tangible Picture of the Gospel

We as mothers are never more like Christ than when we sacrifice ourselves for the good of our children. There is no more evident way in which we do this than when we sacrifice our very bodies for the life of our babies for nine months (and beyond!). When eating the Passover meal with His disciples shortly before He went to the cross, Jesus said, "Take, eat; this is My body which is broken for you; do this in remembrance of Me" (1 Corinthians 11:24). There is such a beautiful correlation between how Christ described His physical sacrifice and the very real way in which our own bodies are broken through pregnancy and childbirth. What an honor we have to so picture Christ and His love in such a real way, to understand even just a hint of what He went through on our behalf. It doesn't always feel like an honor, however! Sometimes we have to grieve the pre-baby body we may have lost. But it is an honor, nevertheless.

A common misconception in our culture today is that your body is ruined by your baby. This is simply untrue. Is your body changed by your baby? Certainly. It is not, however, ruined. In order for your body to have been ruined, something must have happened to render it unable to be used, inefficient, and worthless. We understand this to be the true definition of "ruined" when our child breaks a toy. We say that toy has been ruined, and then we proceed to throw it away. Such is not the case with your post-baby body. Your body is miraculous in its God-given abilities. Your body was designed in such a way so as to be able to conceive, sustain, grow, and bring forth new life. To do so then, and to reap the physical effects of having done so, is not to "ruin" your body. It is to fulfill the design God has placed on it. That's pretty awesome, if you think about it!

So, is it a good idea to take care of ourselves? Is it a good, God-given desire to want to be as attractive to our husbands as possible? Is it OK to work out in an effort to reduce some of the ramifications pregnancy has had on our bodies? Of course! Through it all, however, we need to carry with us a proper understanding of what has taken place in our bodies. We need to view our scars as being a daily reminder of the Savior's scars and our brokenness as a beautiful picture of His brokenness. We can view our post-baby bodies as being gracious reminders from a loving Father of all the ways in which He sacrificed for us. We can illustrate for our children, in some small way, the love and saving sacrifice of God through the loving sacrifice of a mother. We can remember that the reason we have scars is because we live in a fallen world in need of a Savior. And we can point ourselves right back to that Savior each time our eyes fall upon those scars.

PART 4

Lies About Our Children

Motherhood Is a Woman's Highest Calling *Mothering Is Unimportant Work* My Identity Is to Be Found in Being a Mother *I Am to Find My Ultimate Fulfillment in Motherhood* Mommy Guilt Is Just Something I Have to Live With *It's Wrong for Me to Go to God Again and Again After I Fail* Theology Isn't for Moms *I Have to Be a Perfect Mom* I Have to Do it All *I Am Enough* My Children Would Be Better Off Having a Different Mom *I'm a Bad Mom* I'm Selfish If I Have Any "Me Time" *I Need a Lot of "Me Time"* Motherhood Has to Be Hard (And Hard Is Bad!) *I Have to "Keep My Act Together"* I Can't Have a Clean House While Raising Children *My Life Is Passing Me By* *I Am Responsible for My Child's Happiness* I Can't Do This Whole "Mothering Thing" *My Success as a Mom Is Directly Tied to How My Children Turn Out* I Don't Know What It Means to Be a Mom If I Only Have One Child *I Don't Have Time* My Postpartum Body Has to Look a Certain Way *Children Are a Nuisance and an Interruption* Children Are Really Expensive *Children Ruin a Marriage* My Focus Should Be on Rules and Regulations *The "Experts" Know Better How to Raise and Educate My Child Than I Do* The Most Important Thing Is My Child's Education *Good Moms Do "XYZ"* You Have to "Do" Motherhood the Way the Culture Tells You

LIE #25

Children Are a Nuisance and an Interruption

For years now, our culture has lied to us about children. We have been told children are little nuisances who serve as nothing more than interruptions to more important plans, vocations, or endeavors. Sadly, the church has, in recent decades, begun to adopt much the same way of thinking. We have completely forgotten how children are viewed in the Bible, exchanging God's truth about little ones for Satan's lies. Consider, for a moment, the following lies that two mamas see people buying into all the time:

> [People believe] that kids are a nuisance, hindrance, and interruption.
>
> —Sarah

> [A common lie is] that kids are a pain!
>
> —Laura

I love how Rachel Jankovic, busy mama of six kiddos, shoots straight with the truth that combats this pervasive lie: "Motherhood is not a hobby; it is a calling. You do not collect children because you find them cuter than stamps. It is not something to do if you can squeeze the time in. It is what God gave you time for."[26] *Motherhood is what God gave you time for.* Man, if this isn't something I have had to consistently remind myself of throughout the course of writing this book! Though the bulk of this project was written in the mornings while my little ones slept, there were times when Baby James (as Anna calls him) would wake up unexpectedly, right in the middle of my book-writing time. In those moments, I had a choice to make. Was I going to be angry and frustrated that he would dare "interrupt" my writing time, or was I going to believe that, if he had awakened, it must be God's sovereign will that I instead tend to my child's needs in that precise moment? I didn't always make the right choice, let me tell you. By God's grace, however, I am coming more and more to the point of not viewing my children as interruptions in those moments, but as being the God-ordained primary objects of my time in this season of life.

I am beginning to understand that His priorities for my life do not center around my writing or my online ministry. God did not give me time in order to first and foremost be an author (though that is an aspect of the many endeavors to which He has called me). First and foremost, apart from my relationship with the Lord and my husband, when God gave me children, He expected me to redeem my time well, primarily using it to tend to and love on my kids. Other pursuits are perfectly acceptable and admirable in this season if the Lord has called me to them, but if anything, they should be viewed more as interruptions to my time with my children rather than the other way around. This truth hurts sometimes, but it's a truth I need to remind myself of on a daily basis.

"Let the Little Children Come to Me"

If anyone could have felt that children were an interruption, it would have been Jesus. After all, He went about His father's business, ministering to people's needs, proclaiming truth, performing miracles, and freeing folks who were in bondage to sin, deception, and misery. Who had time for children? The Lord did, that's who. He never once viewed children as interruptions. Why not? Because He knew a truth we so often forget—children are important. Far from being nuisances or little pains, they are great blessings (see Psalm 127:3-5). Children are the very future of our world.

We see clear evidence of our Lord's loving heart towards children in Luke 18 where we read:

> Then they also brought infants to Him that He might touch them; but when the disciples saw it, they rebuked them. But Jesus called them to Him and said, "Let the little children come to Me, and do not forbid them; for of such is the kingdom of God. Assuredly, I say to you, whoever does not receive the kingdom of God as a little child will by no means enter it (vs. 15-17).

In the chapters leading up to this passage, we see Jesus busy teaching his disciples, admonishing the Pharisees, healing lepers, and doing a lot of traveling. He was a busy man. The preceding verses in Luke 18 show that Jesus had been in the middle of proclaiming truth in parables when people began bringing little children to Him. No doubt the disciples viewed Jesus' teaching time to be what was most important and this arrival of children on the scene as an interruption. Jesus did not. He eagerly welcomed the children, admonishing the disciples to "not forbid them". Those little children whom the disciples viewed as interruptions, Jesus viewed as important examples of Kingdom living.

I am sad to say I'm often much more like the disciples than I am Jesus. When my children need me when I'm not busy, I'm eager to tend to them. When, however, they interrupt me when I am trying to get work done—either for the blog or around my home—I can easily get thrown into a tizzy and begin responding out of a heart of frustration for having been "interrupted". But I need to renew my mind (Romans 12:2), remembering that in order for children to be interruptions, the implication is that there must be some other more important aspect of life with which they are interfering. When my babies need me when I'm trying to get the laundry done or cook dinner and I get frustrated, it is evidence not of having been "interrupted", but of misplaced priorities. Children are always more important than to-do lists. In this book, we have already looked at the importance of housework and the need we have sometimes to dedicate time to those responsibilities even when our children want us. Though I do stand by what I wrote in that chapter, at the end of the day what is ultimately the very most important endeavor is tending to the needs of our children, not dusting the bookshelves.

Now, does that mean we are at our child's beck and call at all times and must always drop what we are doing the moment they express a need? No, of course not. We are not interested in forming a child-centric home wherein our children tell us to jump and we ask how high. As with everything else, this, too, is a heart issue. What is the condition of your heart? What is being revealed about your priorities when your little ones "interrupt" your work or thwart your plans? Are you viewing your work or your own pursuits as being more important than your children? Are you viewing your children as nuisances and little interruptions or as blessings and rewards whom you were specifically given time to dedicate to raising?

Here's the hard truth: if children are a pain, they usually have their parents to blame. Children, though definitely born with a sin nature, typically are not born as little brats. They are not born as the annoying nuisances some people believe them to be. Typically, when children become little pains like that, it is because of the kind of atmosphere in which they are being raised. Perhaps they are being exposed to bad influences via media and entertainment. It could be that there is a lack of discipline in the home. Maybe they have bad eating and exercise habits and thus do not feel well. Or, as is often the case, maybe they have been made to feel that they are little more than daily interruptions, so they act out in a desperate attempt to get a little attention. You see, the sobering reality is that our children pick up on our opinion of them. When we love and adore them, they know it. When we, accidentally or otherwise, send the message that we believe them to be annoying little interruptions, they pick up on that loud and clear, as well, and begin acting out of that place of hurt.

Do you believe your children to be blessings and rewards in your life? Make sure they know it. The more you show your children just how much you love and treasure them, the more those feelings will grow between you and the less you will be tempted to give in to misplaced priorities and false views. Slow down, ignore the to-do list for a moment, be present, and look deeply into the eyes of your little ones. Get down on the floor and play with them. Snuggle with them on the couch as you read a favorite storybook. Giggle as you color silly pictures or watch funny YouTube videos. Get out the cookie cutters and sprinkles and bake a yummy treat together. The more you do things like this, the more you will feel your delight in your children begin to grow.

After all, it's hard to view your children as nuisances or interruptions when you're baking cookies together and your cute little ones end up with flour all over their noses! Cut out the distractions, take the time to "smell the roses" with your kids, and you will soon find your view of them begin to line up more and more with the Lord's view of them.

Jesus, time and time again, eagerly welcomed children into His presence, taking time out of His busy ministry in order to love and serve them, make them feel important, and teach the disciples to be more like them. If ever we begin to think our children are interrupting our abilities to pursue "more important things", we need to take those thoughts captive, stop being as the disciples who believed Jesus' teaching ministry to be more important than taking a moment to welcome and love on little children, and repent of our false understanding as to the worth of little ones. Children are a blessing, a reward directly from the hand of God to us.

I need to remember that the next time I am tempted to think my children are interrupting me from "more important" work. The fact of the matter is this: if we are moms, our children are not interruptions. Our children are the primary ones for whom the Lord gave us time. If we are moms, these little eternal souls have been entrusted directly into our care, and we have been given time to put to good use in the teaching and training of those souls. No to-do list could ever be more important than that!

LIE #26

Children Are Really Expensive

This lie is ever-growing in our day and age with some of the latest estimates putting the total cost of raising a child from birth to age 17 at $233, 610.[27] Jessica shared her thoughts on this lie:

> [A common lie is that you have to] say goodbye to your money. But if you budget well, you'll have plenty.
>
> —Jessica

Jessica makes an excellent point. In this part of the book, we are dealing with generalities people make about children which are not accurate. It can be incredibly expensive to raise a child if you allow it to be, but as with the other two lies in this section, the choice is ours as to whether or not this lie will prove true in our own lives.

It is sad to hear people lamenting about how expensive children are and then allowing this falsehood to dictate whether or not they will add to their families. If we were more driven by the Word of God rather than the estimates and opinions of man, we would all be a lot better off. The fact of the matter is this: it is a fallacy to make a point-blank statement that "children are really expensive" and that, if you are going to be a parent, you will have to "say goodbye to your money". I understand folks out in the world thinking these things. Christians, however, should know better.

What Does the Bible Say?

As I write this book, we are coming up on the 500th anniversary of the Protestant Reformation which emphasized, among other doctrines, the importance of "Sola Scriptura" or "Scripture Alone". In our modern times, we have begun to drift further and further away from this concept, believing the Bible to be irrelevant for much of daily life. My mission in writing this book is to show you, sweet sister, that this simply is not the case! In His infinite wisdom, God crafted His Word in such a way so that it might address each and every issue which could ever arise in life. This lie we are addressing here is no different.

Children Are a Blessing and a Reward

As we touched on when addressing the previous lie, God places a high value on children, referring to them as blessings and rewards (Psalm 127:3-5). Do we honestly believe that God would describe children in this manner, only for children to then turn out to be super expensive little things that would spiral us into debt during the first seventeen years of their lives? This doesn't even make logical sense, and yet it is what many of us believe. So often we hear couples say they are waiting to start a family until they can "afford kids". Or, when a couple adds another baby to their family, they are eyed suspiciously and sometimes even asked, "Are you sure you can afford another?" While it is important to be financially responsible and a good steward of the money God has entrusted to us, we likewise need to begin viewing children as the blessing and reward that

God says they are, and not as the leech to our banking accounts which the culture views them to be.

We Need to "Seek First the Kingdom"

Much of the problem with today's estimates of how much it costs to raise a child is that they are indicative of the wrong idea we have today that our children must have the latest and greatest toys, clothes, pieces of technology, and experiences. Many of today's children view themselves as being entitled to the newest big thing, and many parents are falling prey to this self-centered mentality. The result is that children are becoming more and more expensive—not because they are inherently so, but because parents are allowing them to be. If children are expensive to raise, it is not the fault of the children. It is the fault of the parent, the one in charge of making the decisions about where the money goes and how exactly it will be spent. Yet again, we see that both parents and children would be better off without this pervasive child-centric mentality that is all the rage today.

Rather than focusing our time, attention, and money on those things which are merely temporary, we need to be focusing instead on that which is eternal. Jesus told us in Matthew 6:19-21, "'Do not lay up for yourselves treasures on earth, where moth and rust destroy and where thieves break in and steal; but lay up for yourselves treasures in heaven, where neither moth nor rust destroys and where thieves do not break in and steal. For where your treasure is, there your heart will be also.'" He went on to say in verse 33, "'But seek first the kingdom of God and His righteousness, and all these things shall be added to you.'"

This is not merely an issue of us needing to find ways to save money as we parent our children. This is a heart issue with eternal ramifications. If we allow our children to dictate where our money goes and how much we are willing to pay for things, their treasure will quickly become laid up on earth rather than in heaven. This is a problem far larger than merely throwing away money on things which are unimportant or finding ourselves in debt. This is a problem at the soul level, a problem which needs to be addressed with the truth of God's Word. We need to be consistently pointing our children back to the Lord and the need we all have for Him—not for some fancy, expensive gadget that will be rendered outdated in six months.

We are Commanded to Be Good Stewards

Another problem with the current trend of children costing their parents upwards of $200,000 to raise is that parents are failing to be good stewards of the money entrusted to them by God. Our money is not our own to be spent however we want. If we have a cent to our name it is because God chose to give it to us. Yes, we may have worked for it, but it still ultimately belongs to the Lord, He gave us the strength and abilities to earn it, and it is our responsibility as stewards to put it to good use.

First Timothy 6:17-19 says, "Command those who are rich in this present age not to be haughty, nor to trust in uncertain riches but in the living God, who gives us richly all things to enjoy. Let them do good, that they be rich in good works, ready to give, willing to share, storing up for themselves a good foundation for the time to come, that they may lay hold on eternal life." When it comes to our finances, we are to: 1) humbly remember they come from the hand of God, 2) trust in God our Provider, 3) be ready to give and willing to share out of the financial benefits God has entrusted to us, and 4) save and be wise with how we handle our finances. Chances are, if we were to be faithful to do these things, we would find that children are not nearly as expensive as we may have assumed.

If our children are costing us over $200,000 each, it is likely because we are going about things the wrong way. I don't know about you, but I see no problem in saving money by buying things second-hand! About ninety-five percent of the clothes, toys, shoes, books, and movies that our children own have come from thrift stores, garage sales, Facebook yard sale pages, CraigsList, used book stores, friends from church, and older cousins. Many of these items have looked brand new when we got them, but we saved a ton of money acquiring them second-hand as opposed to thinking we had to buy everything new. Because of our shopping habits, I get major sticker-shock whenever I am actually in a department store. When you see the kind of retail prices on kids' clothes alone these days, you can quickly see how children could be costing their parents a fortune!

This is not how it has to be, however. We can instead choose to be good stewards of the money entrusted to us by God. We can, as Jessica suggested, purpose to budget well. We can pinch pennies and still have beautiful, like-new possessions. We can save money on the things we need so that more of our finances might be available to better serve others in need of the good news of the gospel. We can use our money in such a way as to "lay up treasure in Heaven" and store up a "good foundation for the time to come." Or we can be downtrodden, believing our children to be costing us a quarter of a million dollars each. We can believe our children to be so expensive that we will never have a retirement fund and never be able to financially serve others. We can believe children to be so expensive that we dare not add another one to our family. It's up to you, mama. What are you going to believe?

Motherhood Is a Woman's Highest Calling *Mothering Is Unimportant Work* My Identity Is to Be Found in Being a Mother *I Am to Find My Ultimate Fulfillment in Motherhood* Mommy Guilt Is Just Something I Have to Live With *It's Wrong for Me to Go to God Again and Again After I Fail* Theology Isn't for Moms *I Have to Be a Perfect Mom* I Have to Do it All *I Am Enough* My Children Would Be Better Off Having a Different Mom *I'm a Bad Mom* I'm Selfish If I Have Any "Me Time" *I Need a Lot of "Me Time"* Motherhood Has to Be Hard (And Hard Is Bad!) *I Have to "Keep My Act Together"* I Can't Have a Clean House While Raising Children *My Life Is Passing Me By* *I Am Responsible for My Child's Happiness* I Can't Do This Whole "Mothering Thing" *My Success as a Mom Is Directly Tied to How My Children Turn Out* I Don't Know What It Means to Be a Mom If I Only Have One Child *I Don't Have Time* My Postpartum Body Has to Look a Certain Way *Children Are a Nuisance and an Interruption* Children Are Really Expensive *Children Ruin a Marriage* My Focus Should Be on Rules and Regulations *The "Experts" Know Better How to Raise and Educate My Child Than I Do* The Most Important Thing Is My Child's Education *Good Moms Do "XYZ"* You Have to "Do" Motherhood the Way the Culture Tells You

LIE #27

Children Ruin a Marriage

There is a dangerous, most unfortunate lie being adopted by both the culture as well as the church these days, and it is the lie that children ruin marriages. Those of us in the church would not admit to believing such a thing in so many words, perhaps, but we are living out that belief on a day-to-day basis when we consistently put our children and their needs ahead of our husbands and marriages. Listen to the wisdom Jessica shared with me on Instagram:

> [It's so common for new moms to hear] 'Say goodbye to your romantic life!' Really?? Says who?? Plan dates, make an effort to keep the spark!
>
> —Jessica

Amen! I love Jessica's passion and could not agree more. As we saw a few lies back, we need to be focusing on our husbands, putting them second only to God, and dedicating time and effort to the cultivation and ongoing strength and growth of our marriages. It doesn't matter what season of mothering we are in; we need to be focusing on our husbands. Precisely how we go about doing so can vary as our children are at different ages and going through different stages. But to do so in some form or fashion is non-negotiable. The Lord gave you your husband before He gave you your children, and your husband is the one you will be left with when the children grow up and leave home. Don't make the mistake of neglecting your marriage in the busy here-and-now. If you do, you will likely wake up one morning wondering who the stranger is beside you in bed, and you may even end up as a statistic, joining the countless other husbands and wives whose thirty plus year marriages ended in divorce after their children left home.

It's so sad to me to see moms who think they have no time for their husbands. Just imagine if their husbands treated them that way! Those women would be crushed and rightfully so. Yet, we excuse this kind of behavior in ourselves because we're "so busy" with the kids. We're so busy doing the good work of feeding, bathing, listening to, and caring for our children that we forget we were called to be helpmeets to our husbands before we were called to be mothers to our children. This unfortunate tendency to place our children above our husbands in level of importance is another one of the rotten fruits produced by the lie we addressed all the way back at the very beginning of this book. After all, if we believe motherhood is a woman's highest calling, then it follows that being a mother is more important than being a wife, and tending to your children is more important than paying attention to your husband.

Does focusing on the importance of marriage, though, mean that we neglect the needs of our kids? Absolutely not! What it does mean is that in the midst of tending to their physical needs we also remember the emotional and spiritual need our children have to be raised in a secure, loving environment where they can see the true beauty of godly marriage lived out in front of them on a daily basis.

To be quite honest, whether or not this lie will prove true in your marriage is completely up to you and your husband. You determine this. It is a lie to say that in general children ruin marriages. They don't. Having children can make a marriage more beautiful, richer, more purposeful, and more intimate as husband and wife now have a tangible, visual, walking-

and-talking, living reminder every day of the love they share. But I must warn you again—this lie can prove true in your marriage if you allow it to. It's all up to you.

How Having Children Can Actually Strengthen a Marriage

Having Kids Deepens Your Love

When you have children, you forever have a beautiful picture of the love that exists between you and your husband. In addition, your love for one another grows as you watch your spouse grow as a person when he takes on the new role of parent. There is something so special about watching your man become a father. It is one of the sweetest things to behold! To see your strapping husband with your sweet baby instantly wrapped around his finger is a precious thing. While it is true that having children can add busyness to your life which can make time alone, date nights, and uninterrupted conversations a bit challenging to have at times, it nevertheless is also true that having children really can deepen your love as husband and wife, making your marriage all the sweeter as you have that daily reminder of the love, intimacy, and union you share as a couple.

Having Kids Brings You Closer Together as You Work Towards a Common Goal

Anytime you are on the same team with someone, working together in a common mission, you grow closer to that person and build a camaraderie. This is the way it is with parenting (providing that you are largely on the same page in terms of your parenting methods, etc.). As you and your husband are in the busy season of parenting, your marriage can still be strengthened if you intentionally allow it to be. As the two of you work together as a team to raise children to the glory of God, your love and support for one another can be strengthened and deepened in truly beautiful ways.

Sex After Children Can Actually Be Better Than Before

Yep, I just went there...because it's true! A lot of women fear that sex after children will be horrible. It is true that for some women, depending on the exact kind of delivery they experienced, sex can be adversely affected. For many women (myself included), however, sex ends up being better after having children than it was before they had kids. If sex was ever painful or uncomfortable for you in the early days of your marriage, a lot of that pain or discomfort may very well go away after your body goes through the changes brought about by pregnancy and childbirth. In addition to the physical benefit which may be produced by having babies, sex can be better emotionally and mentally as the work of parenting brings you and your husband closer together and builds your intimacy in other aspects of your marriage, as well.

God Designed Family to Be This Way

Did you know that God designed marriage and family to be a joyful and beautiful institution? He didn't design marriage to start off amazing only for it to then be ruined by children being brought into the picture. Far from it! Consider the beautiful words of Psalm 128:

> When you eat the labor of your hands, You shall be happy, and it shall be well with you. Your wife shall be like a fruitful vine In the very heart of your house, Your children like olive plants All around your table. Behold, thus shall the man be blessed Who fears the Lord (vs. 2-4).

Far from being a hindrance to the cultivation of a good marriage, children are an integral part of a happy family. We see in this Psalm (much like in the previous Psalm, Psalm 127) that the man who has a wife and children is blessed! He is happy! Clearly, then, it is not inevitable that having children will ruin your marriage, and it is ridiculous for us to think otherwise.

It is true, as we have already touched on, that adding children to the mix can prove challenging to a marriage at times, as parenting can tend to take up a lot of time, energy, and attention. Sometimes it can feel incredibly hard to intentionally focus on your marriage as you should. Such is the nature, however, of things that are worth doing—they do tend to be hard. That doesn't mean, however, that you give up, throw in the towel, and believe parenting to be detrimental to your marriage. It means you fight all the more for the strength of your relationship with your husband, that you become all the more intentional at focusing on your marriage and your spouse. And, through it all, it means remembering that, rather than ruining a marriage, children can actually bring immense joy, depth of intimacy, and love to a marriage. It all depends on whose perspective we will take as our own—the perspective of the culture at large or the perspective of the God who designed marriage and family life. Children, by nature, do not ruin marriages. Parents without the proper Biblical perspective do. What affect, then, will you allow parenting to have on your marriage? The outcome is largely up to you.

Motherhood Is a Woman's Highest Calling *Mothering Is Unimportant Work* My Identity Is to Be Found in Being a Mother *I Am to Find My Ultimate Fulfillment in Motherhood* Mommy Guilt Is Just Something I Have to Live With *It's Wrong for Me to Go to God Again and Again After I Fail* Theology Isn't for Moms *I Have to Be a Perfect Mom* I Have to Do it All *I Am Enough* My Children Would Be Better Off Having a Different Mom *I'm a Bad Mom* I'm Selfish If I Have Any "Me Time" *I Need a Lot of "Me Time"* Motherhood Has to Be Hard (And Hard Is Bad!) *I Have to "Keep My Act Together"* I Can't Have a Clean House While Raising Children *My Life Is Passing Me By* *I Am Responsible for My Child's Happiness* I Can't Do This Whole "Mothering Thing" *My Success as a Mom Is Directly Tied to How My Children Turn Out* I Don't Know What It Means to Be a Mom If I Only Have One Child *I Don't Have Time* My Postpartum Body Has to Look a Certain Way *Children Are a Nuisance and an Interruption* Children Are Really Expensive *Children Ruin a Marriage* My Focus Should Be on Rules and Regulations *The "Experts" Know Better How to Raise and Educate My Child Than I Do* The Most Important Thing Is My Child's Education *Good Moms Do "XYZ"* You Have to "Do" Motherhood the Way the Culture Tells You

PART 5

Lies About Our Parenting Choices

Motherhood Is a Woman's Highest Calling *Mothering Is Unimportant Work* My Identity Is to Be Found in Being a Mother *I Am to Find My Ultimate Fulfillment in Motherhood* Mommy Guilt Is Just Something I Have to Live With *It's Wrong for Me to Go to God Again and Again After I Fail* Theology Isn't for Moms *I Have to Be a Perfect Mom* I Have to Do it All *I Am Enough* My Children Would Be Better Off Having a Different Mom *I'm a Bad Mom* I'm Selfish If I Have Any "Me Time" *I Need a Lot of "Me Time"* Motherhood Has to Be Hard (And Hard Is Bad!) *I Have to "Keep My Act Together"* I Can't Have a Clean House While Raising Children *My Life Is Passing Me By* *I Am Responsible for My Child's Happiness* I Can't Do This Whole "Mothering Thing" *My Success as a Mom Is Directly Tied to How My Children Turn Out* I Don't Know What It Means to Be a Mom If I Only Have One Child *I Don't Have Time* My Postpartum Body Has to Look a Certain Way *Children Are a Nuisance and an Interruption* Children Are Really Expensive *Children Ruin a Marriage* My Focus Should Be on Rules and Regulations *The "Experts" Know Better How to Raise and Educate My Child Than I Do* The Most Important Thing Is My Child's Education *Good Moms Do "XYZ"* You Have to "Do" Motherhood the Way the Culture Tells You

LIE #28

My Focus Should Be on Rules and Regulations

The interesting thing about this lie is that it almost didn't find its way into the book! Clearly the Lord wanted it included, however, because my idea to write about this issue came as we were already in editing mode! Just when I thought the book's content was complete, my mom and I struck up a conversation surrounding observations we have made regarding Christendom today, and that very conversation led to what you will read here. Don't you love how the Lord works?

The State of the Christian Family

As my mom and I discussed the other day, in recent years it has been startling the number of "good Christian people" we have seen fall by the wayside into awful sin. At an alarming rate, everyone from folks who led Christian ministries to folks who were homeschooled and raised in conservative Christian families have publicly fallen. It made me wonder—*Why? What is going on?*

Though there could be many factors leading to this tragedy, my observation has been this: I believe that with many of these folks, the problem has been that they were so extremely sheltered as children with a multitude of "rules" placed upon them, that they never learned how to discern truth for themselves and their hearts may never have been reached with the transforming power of the gospel.

How We Got to This Point

Let's face it—it's scary being a mom. Particularly in our current cultural climate, it can be scary to come to the realization that we are responsible for guarding our little ones as best we can against the evils of this world, preserving their innocence, and guarding their hearts and minds as long as possible. We want nothing more than to see them walking in the truth (3 John 1:4) with their purity whole and intact, and this seems to be increasingly difficult in such a post-Christian culture as the one in which we live.

Parents a couple of decades back picked up on the sobering reality of their responsibility before God as they looked at the increasingly immoral culture around them and began to take seriously their calling to train their children up well. And that was good! The problem, however, came when they made the mistake of choosing the wrong answer to the situation at hand. They looked at the culture that was then only a couple of decades after the sexual revolution and saw the carnage it had left in its wake. Those parents saw the sad aftermath of "sexual freedom" and knew they wanted what would be far better for their kids: God's standard for sexuality and purity. But rather than simply remove themselves and their children from the culture's definition of sex and then land squarely in the arena of the Bible's definition, they ran so hard and so fast from the culture's teachings that they instead landed in the legalistic camp, where not only were their children not supposed to have sex before marriage (i.e. God's actual standard), but they also weren't supposed to spend any time alone before marriage, hold hands, or go out on dates (i.e. legalism). This happens time and time again in the church. We so vehemently reject a philosophy or lifestyle which contradicts God's Word that rather than merely following God's Word itself, we instead, out of fear, act as the Pharisees, adding a plethora of extra rules and regulations in an effort to keep ourselves and our children from stumbling. Sadly, what might begin with good intentions like this oftentimes yields bad results.

To Shelter or Not to Shelter

Homeschoolers are sometimes sneered at and told, "Oh, you're so *sheltered*!", as if that is an insult and being sheltered against the evils of this world is a bad thing. A "shelter", however, is actually a good thing; it is a refuge from the storms of this culture. It is right for us as parents to seek to shelter our little ones from the ways of this world for as long as we can in an effort to preserve their innocence. This is part of our calling. However, the point of that sentence that we need to remember is the little phrase *for as long as we can*. Because here's the deal: sheltering can actually become a bad thing if not gone about the right way!

There comes a time when it is no longer appropriate to so diligently hide our children away from anything and everything our sinful world would try to throw at them. It is certainly true that it is our responsibility as parents to wisely determine what will and will not be allowed into our homes in terms of influences from TV, books and magazines, and access to the internet and smart phones. It is true that our children have been directly entrusted to us by God and that, because of this, we are to diligently guard their little hearts and minds. It hurts our mama hearts to consider the reality that our children will have to become privy to the darkness in this world at some point. But this is a reality we have to nevertheless face. If we don't, our children will be far worse off in the end.

Protecting or Preparing?

What we as moms have to remember is that we are not raising our children to be perpetual children. We are raising them to be adults, to go out and live their lives in the real world, to perhaps marry and have children of their own (and thereby raise the next generation). When we keep this in mind, we see that in order to be lights and live as strong, God-honoring Christians in the midst of a crooked and perverse culture, our children must be prepared to stand on their own two feet, discerning truth for themselves and forming their own convictions. Our children cannot be overly sheltered from the sins and temptations that exist out in the world for the first eighteen years of their lives, and then be expected to stand firm when they go off on their own and the wiles of the devil suddenly come calling.

There is a sense in which we are certainly called to protect our children and their hearts, souls, and minds. But there comes a point when a little of that protecting has to be removed and a little preparing be put in its place. If our children are going to grow up to stand firm in a culture which will seek to tear them down, they will have to have been equipped to be discerning themselves. They will have to be adept at practicing their faith and using their discernment muscles. There is a difference between the preservation of your children's innocence and a failure to actually prepare your children for life. We need to ensure that our children are ready and prepared to stand strong as adults, rather than be blindsided by the world and its entrapments. As with everything else, there is a balance to be had.

Additionally, we need to open our eyes and come to terms with the fact that even when our children are still at home and under our care, the likelihood is that they will at some point be exposed to immorality and darkness in one form or another. We are incredibly naive if we think our children and their innocence are best served by our never alerting them to the evils which abound.

Sally Clarkson made this point well when she said in a recent podcast episode[28] that, at an age-appropriate time, she and her husband intentionally alerted their sons (and their daughters) to the existence of pornography. At first glance, this seems incredibly scary. My first thought is, *If I don't tell my child about this stuff, they'll never know it exists!* Or *Now that they know it exists, they're going to go in search of it out of curiosity, and it'll be all my fault!* But Sally, in her typical, wise way, pointed out that the opposite proved true for them. She and her husband knew that the likelihood was that, at some point, her sons were going to come face to face with pornography (whether in the checkout lane, in an ad popping up on the computer, or from a friend showing it to them), so she wanted them to be prepared ahead of time to know how to react when it happened.

So, what did she and her husband do? They told their sons that pornography exists, put a distaste for it in their mouths by sharing with them the reality that pornography is a victimization and objectification of women (and that most women in that line of work are in it simply because they desperately think it to be the only way they can provide for themselves), and told them what to do if they ever came face to face with it. Sally and her husband pointblank told their sons that if they ever came across pornography, they wanted them to come and tell them. They wanted them to know that they were always welcomed, loved, and able to feel safe coming to their parents no matter what. And you know what? When one of their sons was exposed to the evils of pornography, that's exactly what he did!

Now, what do you think the outcome would have been if Sally and her husband had, out of fear, never told their sons about the evils of pornography, but had instead clamped a heavy rule down on them, telling them that under no circumstances were they ever allowed to access the internet? Not only would that have ultimately not succeeded in preserving them from the evils out there, but it would have rendered their sons unprepared and ineffective in standing against said evils if and when they did appear.

Our focus as moms should not be on rules and regulations. Our focus should be on our child's heart. Proverbs 23:26 illustrates this well when we read, "My son, give me your heart, and let your eyes observe my ways." Slapping a rule or a regulation on a situation will not fix (or prevent) anything. It will simply allow the potential problem to fester, for the heart will have not yet been changed. The truth is that our goal is to reach the hearts of our children, not merely put a band-aid on their outward behavior or issue a hard and fast legalistic rule, naively believing that to be the answer to our desire for our children to lead holy lives.

Should we have house rules as parents? Certainly, we should! But we have to remember two things: 1) The rule must be based solely on Scripture, not on our own fear-based, man-made standards, and 2) The rule must not be viewed as the ultimate preventative to sin in the lives of our children; we must give room for the Holy Spirit to do a heart-work in them through our efforts of consistently pointing them not to a rule, but to a relationship.

I don't know about you, but I am far more interested in the condition of my child's heart than I am his or her outward behavior (and, yes, I actually do mentally repeat that to myself now when I'm dealing with a toddler temper flaring in public!). The reason why can be found in what Jesus said in Matthew 23:25-28:

> "Woe to you, scribes and Pharisees, hypocrites! For you cleanse the outside of the cup and dish, but inside they are full of extortion and self-indulgence. Blind Pharisee,

> first cleanse the inside of the cup and dish, that the outside of them may be clean also. Woe to you, scribes and Pharisees, hypocrites! For you are like whitewashed tombs which indeed appear beautiful outwardly, but inside are full of dead men's bones and all uncleanness. Even so you also outwardly appear righteous to men, but inside you are full of hypocrisy and lawlessness."

I don't know about you, but I don't want whitewashed-tomb children. Ultimately, that's far scarier to me than the realization that my children will one day have to become acquainted with the evils of the world. To think of the possibility that my children could appear perfectly docile and obedient, righteous, clean-cut and always perfectly modest, but in reality be full of hypocrisy, rebellion, lawlessness, and self-indulgence on the inside is incredibly sobering. I would much rather my children act out so that a sin issue in their hearts might be exposed, brought into the light, and dealt with, than have them appear to be perfect and have that sin dwell in secret in the innermost dark recesses of their hearts where Satan can continue his work. As Paul David Tripp has said[29], every time your child acts out it can be viewed as a grace to you—the Lord is providing you with a glimpse into your child's heart and showing you the true nature of it, so that you can address the sin which resides there. What a blessing!

As a mom seeking to raise her children in the nurture and admonition of the Lord, I don't want to live in fear—fear does not come from God (see 2 Timothy 1:7). I want to walk by faith. I don't want to be that authoritarian parent who throws a bunch of rules and regulations around in the false belief that to do so will result in the perfect child. I don't want to be that legalistic Pharisee fearfully adding to God's Word in a desperate attempt to keep my children from sinning. I don't want to be cleverly deceived by Satan into thinking that legalistic standards and harsh rules are the answer (and inadvertently ignore my child's heart just as Satan wants me to!). We need to stop believing rules to be the savior and start entrusting our children to the One who is. We need to realize that all the rules in the world will prove powerless to produce a heart-change in our children, and instead direct our focus to where it matters.

We need to remember the words of God as found in 1 Samuel 16:7:

> But the Lord said to Samuel, "Do not look at his appearance or at his physical stature, because I have refused him. For the Lord does not see as man sees; for man looks at the outward appearance, but the Lord looks at the heart.

May we pattern our parenting after God and how He parents us. Let's focus on the heart—that's precisely where these life and death situations find their beginning. That's where it matters. As Proverbs 4:23 tells us, "Keep your heart with all diligence, for out of it spring the issues of life." All the rules in the world will not be able to form a child into an adult who will live a holy life. When, however, we focus on our child's heart, seeking to impart truth there and guide our children into a relationship with the Father, that is when, by God's grace, we will end up with children who actually want to follow the Lord's commands and live holy lives.

LIE #29

The "Experts" Know Better How to Raise and Educate My Child Than I Do

I wish I could say that this lie is not one commonly believed by Christian moms, but, unfortunately, it is. Marisa and Amber shared their experience with it:

> I was convinced all the 'experts' know better how to raise and educate my children than I do.
>
> —Marisa

> [It's easy to feel] like you have to take everyone's advice to heart.
>
> —Amber

As soon as we find out we're pregnant, our tendency is to rush to the latest book, blog, or parenting course, gleaning the advice and input of the "experts". We research all things related to pregnancy and birth, we read up on all the baby topics (sleep training, when and how to introduce solids, breastfeeding vs. bottle-feeding), and more. This continues on and on throughout the various stages of parenting as our children leave one season and enter another. Now, there is nothing inherently wrong with doing research. In fact, I am definitely a researcher myself and would say that in certain areas (such as those pertaining to labor and delivery, vaccines, feeding babies, etc.) doing your research can be incredibly valuable and important. The problem comes, however, when we begin to think the "experts" have all the answers and forget the access we have to the One who actually does.

The funny thing is that we have this tendency to rush to pick up the latest parenting book from one of the biggest world-renowned experts, when even the "experts" don't all agree! If the "experts" truly knew best, they would not differ from one another in what they are advocating. Some "experts" emphasize the importance of sleep-training and sometimes allowing your baby to "cry it out" in order to learn the skill of "self-soothing". Other "experts" cry foul on this teaching claiming sleep-training to be borderline child abuse, and babies who have been allowed to cry it out to be forever affected mentally. Some "experts" believe that not vaccinating your children is negligence, while others believe actually vaccinating your children is negligence. When I was born, the "experts" were telling parents to have their babies sleep on their bellies in order to avoid choking on spit-up. At other times having infants sleep on their bellies was recommended in order to avoid developing a flat head. Today, "experts" are telling parents they must have their babies sleep on their backs in order to avoid SIDS. When we acknowledge these discrepancies among what is being taught by parenting experts, it quickly becomes clear how false it is to believe they know best. Rather than listening to the experts of parenting, we need to be listening to the Ultimate Expert—the One who created our children and, therefore, truly knows what is best for our own unique little ones.

Where the Church Has Gone Wrong

As I have said repeatedly throughout the course of this book, all of our problems stem from a misunderstanding as to the nature of God's Word. We deem it to be applicable only in issues pertaining to salvation and eternal life when, in reality, the Bible is incredibly relevant to the here and now, as well. The Church made a grave mistake when it took on the belief that reading the Bible and following Jesus is well, fine, and good when it comes to acquiring salvation, but found to be lacking when it comes to addressing the issues that arise in our everyday lives with our families. In this year which marks the 500th anniversary of the Protestant Reformation, I say it is time to have a second Reformation, to hearken the Church back to the concept of Sola Scriptura, and to encourage moms to first pick up their Bibles when they have a parenting question rather than hopping on Amazon to buy some book that is currently topping the charts. God's wisdom as found in His Word never changes; it is never rendered irrelevant (see Numbers 23:19, Hebrews 13:8, James 1:17, Proverbs 30:5, Numbers 24:35, Isaiah 40:8, 1 Peter 1:24-25).

What We Need to Remember

When it comes to battling the lie that the experts know better than we do how to parent or educate our children, there are three things we need to remember:

1. God Uniquely Formed Our Children and Knows Them Best

It is a commonly held—and accurate—assumption that whoever created something knows that creation the best. The company who produced your television drafted an owner's manual for you so that you might know, as they do, the best ways in which to operate your television. The dealership that sold you your car also presented you with an owner's manual straight from the manufacturer which contained the knowledge and insight of the designer of that particular make and model of vehicle. When trying to figure out how to operate your new TV, you would not seek the wisdom of the maker of your car. Likewise, you wouldn't contact your dealership with questions pertaining to why your television won't turn on. To do so would be deemed laughable. Yet this is precisely what we do with our children who are of far more value than any big screen TV or fancy car.

We have direct access to the Creator and Designer of our children, the One who actually formed them (Psalm 139:13-16) and knows everything about them (Psalm 139:1, Romans 8:27, Acts 1:24). Instead of going to the Creator and opening up His instruction manual, however, we jump to read the "wisdom" of some expert somewhere whose insights will likely be challenged by the next expert who comes along and does not know us, our children, or our family dynamics. Why do we make this mistake? I believe it is because we have bought into the lie that the Bible is not applicable to the practical side of our everyday lives. The spiritual, sure, but not the practical. This is most unfortunate because nothing could be further from the truth. As we have seen, God's Word has been given to us specifically because it is living and active (Hebrews 4:12) and able to equip us for every good work (2 Timothy 3:17).

2. God Promises to Give Us Wisdom

Not only does the Lord know each of our own unique children the best, but He promises to share that wisdom with us! He doesn't entrust children to us and then leave us hanging as the deists would have us believe. No. Our God is an intimate, loving, involved Father who delights in helping and guiding His children. He has promised us in James 1:5 that "if any of you lacks wisdom, let him ask of God, who gives to all liberally and without reproach, and it will be given to him." The verse doesn't say wisdom may be given if we pray repetitively for it or ask hard enough. It doesn't say we will be given wisdom if we ask on a day when God happens to feel like bestowing it. We are not told that we can ask, but may or may not receive. No. We are promised, with no "ifs", "ands", or "buts", that when we lack wisdom and cry out to God for it, He will give it to us. In fact, He delights in doing so!

With this promise in mind and with the knowledge that God knows my child better than I or anyone else, I have recently come to a realization. If I am struggling in an area of parenting such as getting my baby to sleep well at night, I don't really need a parenting book about getting your baby to sleep through the night. What I need first and foremost is prayer time with the Father, asking Him to give me wisdom for how to address this sleep situation. I need to be going to Him, asking Him what my baby, with his own unique personality traits and characteristics, needs. I need to ask the Designer of my baby what method would work best for my little guy. I need to seek His wisdom asking Him if sleep-training is what would be in the best interest of my child and, if so, which method to implement. And I need to believe that He will actually answer.

If we do not believe God will provide us with that kind of wisdom, then we don't know the God of the Bible. It is possible, of course, that He may end up giving us a nudge in the direction of picking up one parenting book or another on the issue of sleep-training. He may very well use the words of man to help us along in our journeys. But whether or not He points us in the direction of one of those books, we need to first begin in The Book. Before seeking the wisdom or advice of a friend, pediatrician, or popular blogger, we need to be seeking the wisdom of the Father. We need to be asking what He thinks we should do from His vantage point of knowing everything there is to know about our child. When we ask for the wisdom we need in order to parent well, that is what we will receive. If God has entrusted children into our care, we can rest assured that He will provide the wisdom required to steward those souls well. We only need to ask.

3. God Knows Best

While it is a lie to say that the parenting "experts" know better than we do how to raise or educate our children, it is also a lie to assume that we know best. Neither the parenting expert nor the parent knows best how to train up a child. Only the Creator of that child does. It's important that we not so strongly reject this lie about parenting experts knowing best that we then, in pride, begin believing that we know it all. We always need to be turning to the Lord. And when we do, we can't go wrong. If we rely on ourselves and our own wisdom, however, we will soon find ourselves stumbling around in the dark, wondering how we got ourselves into such a mess. If we want to succeed as moms, we have to start believing God's Word is actually sufficient. We have to always be about the work of seeking His wisdom and opinion on how to raise our children. The Lord has developed a passion in my soul lately to point women back to the Word and the Word alone—so much so that when my friend, Lauren, left me a blog comment saying, "I'm sensing a common theme in your post: 'Read the word!'", it was the most encouraging thing she could have possibly said to me. That is the cry of my heart, mama—that you would be in the Word.

Seek His Wisdom, Mama!

While it is so true that the parenting experts don't know what's best as often as they think they do, the truth is we don't, either. Praise be to God, however, that we are not left there! We are not left to our own devices, our own nearsighted view, or our own man-made wisdom. The Lord has promised to provide us with all the wisdom we could ever need for parenting. All we have to do is ask for it.

So, what will you do, mama, the next time you are facing a parenting dilemma and find yourself at a loss as to what to do? Will you jump on Amazon in desperation, quickly ordering the latest parenting book which promises all the answers? Or will you go to the God who knows your child in and out and has all the answers to any question you could ever think to ask? The choice is yours. Choose carefully.

Motherhood Is a Woman's Highest Calling *Mothering Is Unimportant Work* My Identity Is to Be Found in Being a Mother *I Am to Find My Ultimate Fulfillment in Motherhood* Mommy Guilt Is Just Something I Have to Live With *It's Wrong for Me to Go to God Again and Again After I Fail* Theology Isn't for Moms *I Have to Be a Perfect Mom* I Have to Do it All *I Am Enough* My Children Would Be Better Off Having a Different Mom *I'm a Bad Mom* I'm Selfish If I Have Any "Me Time" *I Need a Lot of "Me Time"* Motherhood Has to Be Hard (And Hard Is Bad!) *I Have to "Keep My Act Together"* I Can't Have a Clean House While Raising Children *My Life Is Passing Me By* *I Am Responsible for My Child's Happiness* I Can't Do This Whole "Mothering Thing" *My Success as a Mom Is Directly Tied to How My Children Turn Out* I Don't Know What It Means to Be a Mom If I Only Have One Child *I Don't Have Time* My Postpartum Body Has to Look a Certain Way *Children Are a Nuisance and an Interruption* Children Are Really Expensive *Children Ruin a Marriage* My Focus Should Be on Rules and Regulations *The "Experts" Know Better How to Raise and Educate My Child Than I Do* The Most Important Thing Is My Child's Education *Good Moms Do "XYZ"* You Have to "Do" Motherhood the Way the Culture Tells You

LIE #30

The Most Important Thing is My Child's Education

I love the name my friend, Jen, assigned to her blog: "Heaven Not Harvard".[30] The name illustrates her heart's desire to focus her attention primarily on raising her daughter to ultimately be a citizen of Heaven, rather than merely a student at Harvard. Jen grasps a truth many of us fail to realize: it is far more important to focus on the condition of our child's soul, seeking to train our little one in the ways of God, than it is to focus on his or her schooling or education.

> [A common lie I see today is that] the most important thing is your kids' education.
>
> —Chrissy

It is very common in both the culture and the church to place an overemphasis on two things: academics and athletics. Many moms are striving to ensure their children receive the best possible education, with the fast track to an Ivy League school being the end goal. Other moms are busy shuffling their children to this sports practice or that game in an effort to see them become Olympic-level in their athletic ability. While being highly educated is certainly important, and athletic prowess can be beneficial to some extent, to tend to our children's souls is far more so.

The Education of the Apostle Paul

Paul gives us his academic background in Acts 22 verse 3: "I am indeed a Jew, born in Tarsus of Cilicia, but brought up in this city at the feet of Gamaliel, taught according to the strictness of our fathers' law." It is quite clear that, humanly speaking, Paul had much to boast of regarding his knowledge and education. In the first century AD, Gamaliel was considered to be one of the leading Jewish teachers, as well as an authority in the Sanhedrin (or "Supreme Court" of Ancient Israel, as it were).[31] To have been educated "at the feet of Gamaliel" would have been viewed in the same way that being educated at Harvard or Yale is today.

What is interesting, however, is that in spite of the preeminence and praise such an education would have clearly afforded Paul, in truth it benefited him little. In fact, it could be said that his education actually did him more harm than good, serving to blind him to the truth of who Jesus was and leading to his persecution of the Church (see Philippians 3:6). It took Christ meeting with him (and literally blinding him!) on the road to Damascus for him to finally see the truth of who the Messiah was. Clearly, receiving a world-renowned education is not all it's cracked up to be!

Sports < Godliness

Now we turn to the issue of sports and why it is a folly for us to place the pursuit of athletics on a higher plane than the pursuit of God and teaching our children theology. In 1 Timothy 4:7-9, Paul writes:

> But reject profane and old wives' fables, and exercise yourself toward godliness. For bodily exercise profits a little, but godliness is profitable for all things, having promise of the life that now is and of that which is

> to come. This is a faithful saying and worthy of all acceptance.

Paul is not against things like physical exercise or sports (the Greek word here is gymnasia, which is where we get our word "gymnasium" and, therefore, denotes athletics). They are not inherently the problem; he even admits that they are somewhat beneficial. The problem is when we pursue them (or anything else!) to the negligence of our pursuit of godliness. Or, to put it another way, the problem is when we idolize sports in our homes, dedicating so much of our children's precious time to games and practices, we leave little time for learning and growing in the things of God.

The reason why what Paul says here is "worthy of all acceptance" is because he is absolutely right—physical exercise and athletics benefit us a little as they tone and condition our bodies. Our bodies, however, will one day die and decay. Our souls, on the other hand, will live forever, rendering the pursuit of godliness far more beneficial to us both in the here and now as well as in eternity.

The Condition of Our Churches

Ronald Reagan once said, "Freedom is never more than one generation away from extinction."[32] The same could be said for many of the churches in our country. Many polls and studies have been conducted in recent years, all showing the same disheartening results: teens and young adults are leaving the church in droves. While there are likely many different reasons for this, I wholeheartedly believe that our incessant pursuit of the idols of athletics and academics is playing a big part in this mass exodus of young people away from the church.

The question is this: is it worth it? Is it worth it to get our children on the fast track to Harvard? Is it worth it to chauffeur them around to this sports activity and that sports activity? Is it worth it to pursue the highest possible academic accolades and the sports trophies and championship statuses? Is all of this worth it if it comes at the cost of your child's soul? I don't think it is.

Again, there is nothing inherently wrong with desiring that your children be highly educated or allowing them to have fun in sports. Each family, however, must prayerfully decide, with the direction and wisdom of God, just how much time and effort they will dedicate to these temporal things. Each family must assess for themselves where their time is being spent and what their calendar reveals them to be prioritizing. Each family must take stock of how educated their children are in theology, how close they are to the Lord, and how much they desire to follow Him. Because the fact of the matter is, if our children spend every waking moment either pursuing academics or athletics, they will likely not grow up to know God, they will not have a deep relationship with Him, they will not know the ends and outs of right theology, and the end result will be that they most likely will leave the church in adulthood. There will be nothing to keep them around, no close relationship with the Lord to tether them to the church.

If we lose much of an entire generation, what then will be the future of the Christian church in America? If the churches in America become largely depleted, what will the impact be on the other countries of the world that are in dire need of missionaries? These are all questions we need to be asking ourselves as parents as we make choices about how our kids will spend their time and in what activities they will be involved. The stakes are high. This is about so much more than whether or not your children should try out for football or pursue that college scholarship. This is about the condition of their souls, their eternity, and the future of the world.

Reject Satan's lie that your child's education or athletic pursuits are what is most important. Don't allow him to distract you with temporal things which are of little to no lasting importance while your child's soul goes by untended to. Follow in the footsteps of my friend, Jen, and work in such a way in your mothering that your child might be prepared for Heaven, not Harvard.

Motherhood Is a Woman's Highest Calling *Mothering Is Unimportant Work* My Identity Is to Be Found in Being a Mother *I Am to Find My Ultimate Fulfillment in Motherhood* Mommy Guilt Is Just Something I Have to Live With *It's Wrong for Me to Go to God Again and Again After I Fail* Theology Isn't for Moms *I Have to Be a Perfect Mom* I Have to Do it All *I Am Enough* My Children Would Be Better Off Having a Different Mom *I'm a Bad Mom* I'm Selfish If I Have Any "Me Time" *I Need a Lot of "Me Time"* Motherhood Has to Be Hard (And Hard Is Bad!) *I Have to "Keep My Act Together"* I Can't Have a Clean House While Raising Children *My Life Is Passing Me By* *I Am Responsible for My Child's Happiness* I Can't Do This Whole "Mothering Thing" *My Success as a Mom Is Directly Tied to How My Children Turn Out* I Don't Know What It Means to Be a Mom If I Only Have One Child *I Don't Have Time* My Postpartum Body Has to Look a Certain Way *Children Are a Nuisance and an Interruption* Children Are Really Expensive *Children Ruin a Marriage* My Focus Should Be on Rules and Regulations *The "Experts" Know Better How to Raise and Educate My Child Than I Do* The Most Important Thing Is My Child's Education *Good Moms Do "XYZ"* You Have to "Do" Motherhood the Way the Culture Tells You

LIE #31

Good Moms Do "XYZ"

It seems so crazy to say this at this point, but it's true: I never planned to write this book. Have you ever had something happen in your life that you just knew was the Lord's doing and not your own? You know, a real-life case of Proverbs 16:9 ("A man's heart plans his way, but the Lord directs his steps") really coming alive for you? That is exactly what this book has been for me! This is actually not the book I set out to write. The book you are now reading began back in the spring as simply an article idea for my blog, and the Lord positively exploded it from there.

The book I planned to write (which will now be my second book unless the Lord has yet another idea for me to pursue first!) was on the topic of the mommy wars and the many ways in which they are adversely affecting the church. For this reason, I have been looking forward to battling the lie we are addressing now! It's a lie with which many moms struggle (myself included), as illustrated by the responses I got from several different moms—responses which all deal with one side or another of this very lie:

> [I've believed] that 'good moms' do xyz- whatever xyz is. From what we feed our kids to how much time we spend with them, etc.
>
> —Heather

> [I've seen many believe the lie] that certain choices (that aren't even salvation issues) make or break us as Christians.
>
> —Amber

> My biggest thing was discipline. Thinking that there was one right way. It took me years to figure out that you can't discipline all your kids the same. What worked well for one didn't always work for the others. I wish someone had explained that to me way earlier.
>
> —Natalie

> Sometimes we want to believe in a formula for a quick fix or a foolproof strategy to our motherhood.
>
> —Lena

> [A common lie is] that you have to breastfeed your kids in order for them to be healthy. Sometimes it is out of our control.
>
> —Becca

All of these lies center around the same thing: the onslaught of the mommy wars in our day. They all center around the mistaken belief that "good moms" make particular choices in parenting: they all feed their children a certain way, train their children a certain way, and make particular choices regarding things like vaccines, whether or not to circumcise, whether or not to co-sleep, and when to turn the car seat around from being rear-facing. Oh, and if you do not do things the way those "good moms" would deem to be the "right" way, they will look down their noses at you.

Such is the ridiculous, but pervasive, nature of the mommy wars and, in turn, the nature of all too many Facebook groups, mommy forums, and, yes, even churches. When you are told you are not a Christian because you don't vaccinate your children (or told you are not a Christian because you do), it is representative of a much larger problem. I wish these were made-up scenarios, but, unfortunately, they are not. Two friends of mine were each told one of these very lies. Another friend of mine ended up even changing churches because of the kind of treatment she was receiving from a fellow mom who disagreed with her parenting choices. This should not be, ladies!

Going Back to the Word of God

From where do all these heightened emotions, judgment calls, and feelings of condemnation which make up the mommy wars come? I would say they stem directly from a shelving of the Word of God in exchange for the wisdom of man. Yet again, we have believed (whether subconsciously or otherwise) that God's Word is not all that relevant to our everyday lives. As a result, we are relying on our own research and what we learn from the "experts" online.

Now, don't get me wrong—I am very much in favor of research, as I have already said. I believe it is super important to be well-researched as a mom, particularly in areas pertaining to your child's health and wellbeing. However, when we flock first to the recommendations of man, believing them to be the ultimate standard and source of wisdom, what happens is that we have a tendency to quickly become emotionally attached to the answers we have found through our research and begin disdaining anyone who does not do things the way our research has told us is best.

This is evidenced by the ridiculous accusation faced by my friends that they were "not Christians" because of their choices in the area of vaccinations. Such an idea exemplifies several problems in the church today, not the least of which is a clear misunderstanding of the gospel and what constitutes being a Christian. As we have seen repeatedly throughout the course of this book, being a Christian is based solely on you placing faith and trust in Jesus and what He accomplished on the cross. It has nothing whatsoever to do with whether or not you vaccinate your kids. If we think it does, we are guilty of the sobering mistake of adding to God's Word, which is something the Lord takes very seriously (see Deuteronomy 4:2, Deuteronomy 12:32, Revelation 22:18). While our parenting choices in these various areas are important, they do not, as Amber said, "make or break us as Christians."

The mommy wars are a result of us making mountains out of mole hills, plain and simple. We have taken secondary issues—what we feed our children, how they learn to sleep through the night, whether or not they are vaccinated—and put them on par with true Scriptural commands. In doing so, we have also committed the opposite mistake and made mole hills out of mountains, forgetting the commands of God because we are so distracted by the temporal issues of where our babies sleep and whether or not their car seat is still rear-facing when they are three years old. This is not to say that these other parenting issues are not important. What it does mean, however, is that we need to stop making the mistake of applying a level of importance to them which they were never meant to possess.

It's time we hearken back to the Word of God, ladies. We need to take back a portion of the time we have given to research and instead dedicate that time to Bible study. If we do, I believe we will start to see a dramatic reduction in the number of mommy war cases in the church. We will grow in our humility, develop more love for fellow moms, and understand what truly is and is not most important. The lie we are addressing that "good moms do xyz" will then naturally go away in the process!

What Are You Trusting In?

The problem with a lot of these lies (such as the one Becca shared that your babies must be breastfed in order to be healthy) is that they point to the fact that we are not placing our trust in God, but rather in what we do as moms. Is it true that some parenting choices may be better than others? Is it true that breastfeeding yields quite a few health benefits? Yes, both of those are true. The Lord's care of our children, however, is not tied to our ability to breastfeed or to the choice we make about vaccines. Our God is sovereign even over the way our children are fed and other parenting choices we make. I have a sweet friend who has been unable to breastfeed any of her three children due to a health issue, but do you know what? Her little ones are perfectly healthy. God is just good that way! The question is, do we believe He is good? Do we trust Him? Or are we trusting in ourselves and the lives we lead?

Psalm 20:7 says, "Some trust in chariots, and some in horses; but we will remember the name of the Lord our God." I don't want to be one of those who trusts in chariots (the equivalent in our day might be the perfect time to switch around a child's car seat or the perfect way to handle vaccine decisions). I want to instead trust in the good care of a loving Father. I want to trust in our sovereign God and His powerful name.

The mommy wars do nothing but turn us into the kind of Pharisees described in Luke 18:9 "who trusted in themselves that they were righteous, and despised others". This is precisely what happens when we, as the Pharisees, add our own beliefs and preferences to the Word of

God. The truth is that a lot of the fear, anxiety, judgment, and guilt we experience in motherhood would begin to melt away if we simply knew God's Word, believed it to be true, and placed our trust solely in the Lord.

Live the Life God has Called YOU To

When we believe that "good moms" do [fill in the blank], we may also end up believing that we need to be just like those other moms, living our lives exactly the way they do. We end up placing heavy burdens on our backs as we try to fit into another person's mold. What we have to remember, however, is that God has not called us to live someone else's life; He has called us to live the life He has entrusted to us. We have been equipped for the good works to which He has called *us*—not the life or calling of our sisters-in-Christ. We oftentimes say things like, "Oh, I can't imagine doing what she's doing", and it could be precisely because God hasn't called us to do what that other mom is doing. As a military wife, I oftentimes hear people say, "Oh, I could never be a military wife!" That is because He has not called you to be one. If He ever did, He would strengthen and equip you for that work. That is not to say that it wouldn't still be incredibly hard at times, but you would find that you could do it.

We need to be careful to stay in our own lanes, mamas. We know that when driving we need to focus on the lane we're in and not the one we aren't—otherwise, our focusing on the other person's lane could result in a fatal head-on collision. Likewise, we need to focus on the lane God has placed us into in life, not our fellow mama's lane. We need to focus on where He has us going, not the journey and destination of someone else. We need to "in all [our] ways acknowledge Him, and He will direct [our] paths" (Proverbs 3:6).

Another issue with this "good moms do xyz" idea is that, oftentimes, the qualifications we place on moms are not based on God's Word. When we spread around this idea, the "xzy" is typically not a true Biblical standard such as, *Good moms read the Bible with their kids.* Instead, we are basing our qualifications of a good mom on man-made expectations such as *Good moms feed their kids all organic foods* or *Good moms color with their kids every day.* We would do well to remember that the Bible does not put great emphasis on moms throwing their kids elaborate Pinterest-worthy birthday parties or planning out elaborate crafts for their kids to do, but on loving their children (Titus 2:4) and training them up in the ways of God (Deuteronomy 6:6-7, Proverbs 22:6, Ephesians 6:4). Pinterest-inspired activities are great, but we mustn't allow the fact that so-and-so planned more such activities for her kids than we did for ours to distract our attention from what truly matters most.

In addition, as Natalie shared above, we need to understand that there is no one-size-fits-all way to parent, though the lie we are addressing here would have us think there is. Each child in each family is so incredibly different and has been hand-designed by God to be unique and to fulfill a unique purpose. When we understand this, it becomes clear just how foolish it would be for us to expect all moms everywhere to hold to the exact same standard of discipline or training in their parenting that we do. To do so would be incredibly unfair and would do fellow moms and children a terrible disservice.

The same goes for the idea that we should, as Lena shared, find the perfect formula or strategy for our mothering. This is what we all want as moms. When a problem arises with one of our children, we want the easy way out. We want to quickly find the perfect method or strategy or answer to take care of the problem once and for all (and be able to enforce said formula on all other mamas!). What this does is chip away at our dependence upon Christ, keeping us from seeking Him in faith for the answers we need for our journey of motherhood. The reality is that the

Lord has all the answers we could ever need. All we have to do is seek them!

Good Moms Imitate Christ!

When we base our view of what a good mom is on the expectations and standards of man, we end up in the wrong comparison game. There is but one comparison "game" we should be playing: we should be comparing ourselves to God, seeking to "be imitators of God as dear children" (Ephesians 5:1). The only other time in the Scriptures that we are encouraged to do things as someone else does is when Paul said in 1 Corinthians 11:1 that we should imitate him as he imitated Christ. This admonition was all about following his example of day-to-day Christian living. It wasn't about Pinterest living or crunchy living or any of the other traps we can fall into of believing earthly things to be more important than they really are. It was about living in accordance with what the Bible actually does say is important, not what our world thinks is important.

All these other areas of parenting are decisions each individual family must make according to the wisdom God gives them. These decisions will vary from parent to parent and rightfully so, for the Lord will show each family what is best according to the unique makeup and dynamics of that particular family. Our Lord knows the interests, needs, and personalities of us and our children, which is why it is so important not to seek the wisdom of man, but the wisdom of God. There is so much freedom in this, mamas! No longer do we have to succumb to the expectations and values of the world or even of our fellow church members. We need only to live according to the Lord's plan for us and our families. So, remember this—

Good moms:

- are about the business of imitating Christ, not the women on social media.
- are about the business of seeking the wisdom of God and trusting His leadership, more than the "perfect" parenting method or man-made formula.
- are about the business of training their children in the ways of God, not sticking their noses in the affairs of other moms.
- are about the business of studying theology more than they are studying all the "right" ways of feeding, dressing, or teaching their kids (as important as those things may be).
- are about the business of seeking answers from God more than they are answers from others.

That's what it means to be a good mom, sweet reader. Those are the things which are important in God's eyes. You no longer have to live according to the beliefs of this culture about what constitutes a good mom. You no longer have to live up to the long "XYZ" list of what "good moms" do. You are free to operate in the unique path that has been paved for you by God (Proverbs 3:5-6). You are free to live out the good news of the gospel in your everyday life (John 8:32, Galatians 5:1). You, sweet mama, are free.

Motherhood Is a Woman's Highest Calling *Mothering Is Unimportant Work* My Identity Is to Be Found in Being a Mother *I Am to Find My Ultimate Fulfillment in Motherhood* Mommy Guilt Is Just Something I Have to Live With *It's Wrong for Me to Go to God Again and Again After I Fail* Theology Isn't for Moms *I Have to Be a Perfect Mom* I Have to Do it All *I Am Enough* My Children Would Be Better Off Having a Different Mom *I'm a Bad Mom* I'm Selfish If I Have Any "Me Time" *I Need a Lot of "Me Time"* Motherhood Has to Be Hard (And Hard Is Bad!) *I Have to "Keep My Act Together"* I Can't Have a Clean House While Raising Children *My Life Is Passing Me By* *I Am Responsible for My Child's Happiness* I Can't Do This Whole "Mothering Thing" *My Success as a Mom Is Directly Tied to How My Children Turn Out* I Don't Know What It Means to Be a Mom If I Only Have One Child *I Don't Have Time* My Postpartum Body Has to Look a Certain Way *Children Are a Nuisance and an Interruption* Children Are Really Expensive *Children Ruin a Marriage* My Focus Should Be on Rules and Regulations *The "Experts" Know Better How to Raise and Educate My Child Than I Do* The Most Important Thing Is My Child's Education *Good Moms Do "XYZ"* You Have to "Do" Motherhood the Way the Culture Tells You

LIE #32

You Have to "Do" Motherhood the Way the Culture Tells You

As we have seen throughout the course of this book, both secular culture and church culture alike have been guilty of deceiving us in various ways. Anytime we are following after a fallible human being rather than diligently seeking the truth of God's Word for ourselves, there is the possibility for deception and error. Tami shared with me how she has struggled with this very issue:

> I believed for 17 years that I couldn't stay home with my children or homeschool them. Working all that time, I finally came home to raise my youngest. [For years, I bought into] lies from culture about what a woman should do and what my parents and husband expected of me.
>
> —Tami

Tami is definitely not alone in this struggle. As women living in this day and age, we are taught from childhood that we should pursue careers, never rely on a man, not prioritize having children, and, if we do, certainly not plan to stay home with them. If you grew up, as I did, dreaming of being a wife and stay-at-home mom one day, you are thought of as being weird, behind-the-times, or perhaps even a little delusional. From our earliest days, we have all these voices coming at us as to what we should do with our lives, what our marriages should look like if we do get married, what role our motherhood should play, what our "career" plans should be in the midst of marriage and family, and more.

This is not what the Lord intended for His children, however. He does not want to see us bombarded with cultural expectations and "shoulds", feeling pulled in every direction by folks on every side who each want us to do something different with our time. In fact, the Lord gave us His Word precisely so that we might be freed from all this! Our Lord, as our Designer, knows what is best for us; He knows what kind of living is in our best interests as women. So, He gave us His Word! He gave us His inspired, unchanging Word that we might have access to the truth which sets us free (John 8:32) and might know how we ought to live (1 Timothy 3:14-15). No longer do we have to listen to all the voices out there or try to please all the people. There is but one voice to listen to, and that is the Lord's. There is but one person we should be concerned with pleasing, and that is God. There is but one opinion that matters, and that is our Heavenly Father's. When we understand that, we will begin to taste of the freedom which comes from rejecting the expectations of man in order to simply follow Christ instead (see Matthew 11:28-30).

Throwing Off the Culture's Demands

As Christians, we need to be living in freedom from the culture's demands. We need to stop listening to all the voices out there and instead be sheep who listen only to their Shepherd's voice (John 10:27).

We Are Called to a Different Standard

As Christians, we have a tendency to forget that we are called to actually follow Christ. We place saving faith and trust in Him, and then we sometimes think that that's all there is to it, as if God's Word is crucial for salvation but not sufficient for life's daily decisions. We sometimes think that in the day-to-day issues and struggles of life, we are left to our own devices to determine for ourselves what is best. I hope by this point in the book, however, you are seeing that this simply is not the case. We are not saved to then be right back where we were, dependent on the teachings or expectations of the culture around us.

The truth is that we have been called to be holy as the Lord is holy (see 1 Peter 1:16, Leviticus 11:44). The word for "holy" in these passages literally means "sacred, set apart, consecrated".[33] When we were saved, we were consecrated and made to live in a way that is set apart from this world and its priorities. We are called to live now in a way "worthy of the gospel of Christ" (Philippians 1:27). We can only do that, however, if we let go of the standards placed on us by the culture, rejecting them so that we might be free to follow our Lord's standards instead.

The Double-minded Man Is Unstable in All His Ways

What happens when the Christian places one foot in the Bible and what it says, and the other foot in the world and what it says? He (or she) becomes "unstable in all his ways" (James 1:8). Because the Bible's teachings and the culture's teachings are often at war with one another, we deceive ourselves when we believe we can be faithful to both. It is a complete impossibility, and if we persist in trying to live that way, every aspect of our lives will be adversely affected. We will feel ourselves to be in a constant state of spiritual tug-of-war as each worldview fights to gain the upper hand.

If we want to be strong, bold, visionary, purposeful, and on a solid foundation in our Christian walk, in our marriages, in our mothering, and in life in general, we are going to have to forever let go of the culture's teachings and wholeheartedly embrace the Lord's. If we do so, we will begin to see great fruit being produced in our lives as we wholeheartedly follow Him.

Rest Is Found in the Old Paths

In Jeremiah 6:16 we read, "Thus says the Lord: 'Stand in the ways and see, and ask for the old paths, where the good way is, and walk in it; then you will find rest for your souls.'" The culture's way brings stress, lengthy to-do lists, unending expectations, a hundred and one hats to wear and balls to juggle, and feelings of overwhelm and confusion. The old path, however, brings good, it brings rest, and it brings life and peace, for it is the way in which our souls were created to go. It perfectly suits us and our families, having been designed by the One who designed us.

We need to stop looking to the culture for our answers. We need to stop looking to the culture for our callings. We need to stop looking to the culture for our direction, our wisdom, and our priorities. We need to instead turn back, look for the old path, and walk in it. This is the only way we will be free from the lies and burdens our culture regularly throws at us.

A Word to Wives

I do want to make one note here in regards to wives and their God-given responsibility to submit to their husbands. Tami mentioned how she lived for years according to lies about what her husband expected of her. One important thing to say here is that we are called to submit to our husbands in everything, except for in any case in which they are calling us to sin (see Ephesians 5:22-24, Colossians 3:18, and Titus 2:5). This is where knowing what God's Word actually says is so crucially important because the passages in Ephesians 5 and Colossians 3 speak to us submitting to our husbands in everything "as unto the Lord" and "as is fitting in the Lord". Clearly, it is not fitting to submit when someone calls us to sin. It is only in an instance such as that, however—an instance where a husband tells his wife to do something which is clearly contradictory to the Word of God—that a wife is then free to disregard her husband's wishes. In all other instances, however, a wife is commanded by God to submit herself to the leadership of her husband. The only exception being when dealing with an area of actual sin—not of mere personal preference, opinion, or desire on our part.

So, while it is true that we do not have to "do" motherhood the way the culture tells us to, we do need to submit to our husband's wishes in the area of mothering, providing that doing so would not result in us sinning. If our husband desires for us to work part-time, that is what we should do. If our husband prefers that we not homeschool, as hard as it might be for us to send our kids to school, that is what we should do. This doesn't mean it's easy to go against what we might think is best in mothering in order to submit to our husband's leading. But it does mean we are being faithful to God's way of doing things as part of the design He has set up for how a family operates best.

Does this mean a wife can't share her thoughts with her husband or that a husband should not listen to his wife's point of view? Of course not! Husbands have their own roles they are commanded to fulfill (e.g., loving their wives as Christ loved the church, dwelling with them in understanding, laying down their lives for their wives, etc.). The marriage relationship is an equal partner/equal partner relationship, not a parent/child one. What this does mean, however, is that at the end of the day, after a husband has thoroughly listened to and considered his wife's point of view, if he still feels that his way would be best for their family, a wife is called to willingly submit to that.

Again, that's not to say this is always easy! When a mama bear is convinced she knows what is best for her cubs but has to submit to her husband's leadership, it takes a lot of strength and fortitude to be able to do so! But, ultimately, it comes down to trusting in the plan of the God who set up this design in the first place. Do we trust God? Do we believe He will lead and direct our family, placing us in the path wherein we should go? Do we believe that because He has crafted a husband lead/wife submit design for marriage and family, He will lead our families through our husbands? If we say we believe God's Word, we have to answer yes to these questions. Because God has called the husband to lead, it makes perfect sense that He will ultimately lead the family through that husband and what He calls him to do (there have been so many amazing examples of this in my own family!). We can rest in that. Ladies, we can trust in the good, kind, loving, all-wise heart of God. This does not come naturally and it may not be easy, but it is possible with our Lord's help.

Whose Voice Will You Listen To?

So, mama, it is up to you. Will you listen to the voice of culture, bending your ear and crafting your to-do lists and priorities according to what the world values and says is important? Or will you listen to the voice of the God who made you, who knows you inside and out, who knows what is best for you and your family, and who came that you might have abundant life? While the culture seeks to heap burdens upon your shoulders of what you "must do" in your mothering, making you feel as if you have to craft your motherhood according to its lofty expectations, our Lord is so different. He is so gentle with us, mamas. The culture is not gentle with us, we are not gentle with ourselves, and sometimes not even the church is gentle with us. But He is. I love the word picture of Isaiah 40:11 so much: "He will feed His flock like a shepherd; He will gather the lambs with His arm, and carry them in His bosom, and gently lead those who are with young."

Our Lord is gentle, mama. Turn to Him when you are weary in your mothering. Turn to Him when you have doubts and fears as a mom. Turn to Him when you have questions about how to mother well or what you should be doing as a mom. He is not in the business of placing heavy burdens upon your shoulders. His yoke is easy and His burden is light (Matthew 11:28-30). He is not in the business of weighing you down with to-do lists. He desires for you to remember that in quietness and rest is your strength (Isaiah 30:15). He is not in the business of confusing you, making it unclear what you are to do, or leaving you in the dark at the mercy of the culture and whatever it tells you to do. He is a God of order (1 Corinthians 14:33, 40), gives wisdom in abundance (James 1:5), and directs your paths (Proverbs 3:6).

Rest in these truths today, mama. You do not have to pattern your mothering after what the culture expects of you. You are free to pattern your mothering after the wisdom, freedom, insight, and loving design of our all-wise, gracious Creator. Christ came that you might be free, that you might live in bondage no longer, and that you might be able to stand in liberty before Him (Galatians 5:1). Live in that freedom, mama. It is yours.

Motherhood Is a Woman's Highest Calling *Mothering Is Unimportant Work* My Identity Is to Be Found in Being a Mother *I Am to Find My Ultimate Fulfillment in Motherhood* Mommy Guilt Is Just Something I Have to Live With *It's Wrong for Me to Go to God Again and Again After I Fail* Theology Isn't for Moms *I Have to Be a Perfect Mom* I Have to Do it All *I Am Enough* My Children Would Be Better Off Having a Different Mom *I'm a Bad Mom* I'm Selfish If I Have Any "Me Time" *I Need a Lot of "Me Time"* Motherhood Has to Be Hard (And Hard Is Bad!) *I Have to "Keep My Act Together"* I Can't Have a Clean House While Raising Children *My Life Is Passing Me By* *I Am Responsible for My Child's Happiness* I Can't Do This Whole "Mothering Thing" *My Success as a Mom Is Directly Tied to How My Children Turn Out* I Don't Know What It Means to Be a Mom If I Only Have One Child *I Don't Have Time* My Postpartum Body Has to Look a Certain Way *Children Are a Nuisance and an Interruption* Children Are Really Expensive *Children Ruin a Marriage* My Focus Should Be on Rules and Regulations *The "Experts" Know Better How to Raise and Educate My Child Than I Do* The Most Important Thing Is My Child's Education *Good Moms Do "XYZ"* You Have to "Do" Motherhood the Way the Culture Tells You

LMB

Go Forth in Grace and Truth, Mama!

Oh, sweet mama, I cannot believe we have come to the end of our journey together in the pages of this book. It has gone by so quickly! It has been my absolute honor and joy to come alongside you, discovering and walking out the truth of God's Word, seeing how it combats the lies of Satan, and learning, together, how to live in the freedom Christ won for us.

With each truth I have sought to teach you in this book, please do not simply "take my word for it". Instead, be as the Bereans were (see Acts 17:11), and take everything I have written to you and compare it to the truth of God's Word to see if it be accurate and acceptable. That has been my goal all along—not to make you into little robots who buy into everything I say hook, line, and sinker, but to really get you thinking. My goal with this book has been to open your eyes to just how applicable God's Word is to each and every issue that arises in your life, every lie that enters your head, every struggle you face as a mom. My hope is that once your eyes have been opened to the relevancy of the Bible, you will be equipped through what you have read here to begin taking your every thought captive and comparing everything you believe to the truth of God's Word. Then, my prayer is that you will be willing to let go of the lies, and walk in freedom and truth. After all, it is the truth which sets you free!

When mommy guilt begins to weigh you down, I pray you will remember that, as my friend Tina says, "Our scars are not who we are; His scars are." When you are tempted to believe that you are enough, I pray that you will remember instead that He is, and therein find your strength and the power needed for this journey of mothering. When you start believing your postpartum body is ruined, I hope you remember it actually serves as a beautiful picture of the gospel. When you start thinking the experts know what is best, I pray you remember that you have direct access 24/7/365 to the One who actually does. When you are told that motherhood is your highest calling, I want you to remember that being a child of God and ambassador of Christ is actually your highest calling and understand this is what gives motherhood its significance. When you begin to think what you are doing with your children is unimportant, mundane, and trivial, I hope you remember that you are altering the course of nations. When you are missing the church service yet again because you have to stand out in the hall with a crying baby, I hope you are comforted with the realization that, in that moment, that is your "reasonable service" (Romans 12:1). When you feel crushed under the weight of having to be the perfect mom, I hope you remember that your job is simply to point your children to a perfect Savior. When you are fed the lie that children ruin marriages and leave you with no time for your husband, I pray you fight back and give your marriage the attention it deserves. And, when the going gets tough, when you are exhausted, when motherhood is hard, when you feel as if your children would have been better off with a different mom, I hope you remember the beautiful words of Zephaniah 3:17 and embrace them as your own:

> The Lord your God in your midst, The Mighty One, will save; He will rejoice over you with gladness, He will quiet you with His love, He will rejoice over you with singing.

The Lord is for you, mama, and has fully equipped you for the high and holy calling of motherhood. You've got this! You can do it! I am cheering for you all the way!

So, what do you say? Let's do this!

With much love, grace, and tons of cheerleading,

Rebekah

Motherhood Is a Woman's Highest Calling *Mothering Is Unimportant Work* My Identity Is to Be Found in Being a Mother *I Am to Find My Ultimate Fulfillment in Motherhood* Mommy Guilt Is Just Something I Have to Live With *It's Wrong for Me to Go to God Again and Again After I Fail* Theology Isn't for Moms *I Have to Be a Perfect Mom* I Have to Do it All *I Am Enough* My Children Would Be Better Off Having a Different Mom *I'm a Bad Mom* I'm Selfish If I Have Any "Me Time" *I Need a Lot of "Me Time"* Motherhood Has to Be Hard (And Hard Is Bad!) *I Have to "Keep My Act Together"* I Can't Have a Clean House While Raising Children *My Life Is Passing Me By* *I Am Responsible for My Child's Happiness* I Can't Do This Whole "Mothering Thing" *My Success as a Mom Is Directly Tied to How My Children Turn Out* I Don't Know What It Means to Be a Mom If I Only Have One Child *I Don't Have Time* My Postpartum Body Has to Look a Certain Way *Children Are a Nuisance and an Interruption* Children Are Really Expensive *Children Ruin a Marriage* My Focus Should Be on Rules and Regulations *The "Experts" Know Better How to Raise and Educate My Child Than I Do* The Most Important Thing Is My Child's Education *Good Moms Do "XYZ"* You Have to "Do" Motherhood the Way the Culture Tells You

Let's Continue the Conversation!

I have so enjoyed traveling with you through the pages of this book, dear reader. In fact, I really don't want our time together to end! So, here is what I propose: come find me on social media!

Let's continue to sort through these lies we have been believing, learn the truth of God's Word, encourage each other, and grow in the freedom Christ has provided for us. To that end, I have a companion Bible study in the works for you that will release March 30, 2018 (at the same time the print version of this book comes out)! If you would like to dig deeper into the truths we have been studying in *Lies Moms Believe* and find additional, practical ways to apply them to your own unique life, I welcome you to check out this study. In it, we will continue to see how God's Word successfully refutes the lies we moms are believing. Through an emphasis on both the stories of men and women in the Bible as well as direct teachings from the Lord, we will have our minds renewed by His truth as we take what He has said and watch it make a difference in our lives! Additionally, I have created a private FB Group just for you! You are invited to join the Moms Living Free group on Facebook, where you will be able to meet other like-minded mamas who are traveling this journey of motherhood right alongside you and, together, be encouraged in your walk with the Lord. We can't wait to see you there and have the chance to get to know you better! This will be a private, safe place for us to share our struggles, bear one another's burdens, pray for each another, rejoice in each other's victories, and just enjoy Christian fellowship. So, come join us, won't you?

You can also find me on Instagram: @rebekahhargraves. If this book has encouraged or helped you, it would be such a blessing to hear about that! Please feel free to DM me, tag me in your post about the book, or use the hashtag #liesmomsbelieve to let me know how the book has impacted your life.

And, finally, let's share the love! If the Lord has graciously allowed this book to make a difference in your life, would you please consider leaving a quick review of it on Amazon? That simple act helps immensely when it comes to getting the word out about the book and helping other moms to easily find it and hopefully be encouraged themselves. Just think of this as your way of partnering with me in this ministry! Thank you, friend.

P.S. Be sure to head to the blog to snag your "Living the Mom-Life Free From Lies" coffee mug and daily be reminded of the freedom Christ has for you! Oh, and while you're there, sign up for the monthly newsletter—that is where you will be kept up to date on new books I'm working on, launch team opportunities, and special discount codes for subscribers only!

Notes

1. http://www.quoty.org/quote/3849, accessed July 31, 2017

2. http://www.motherteresa.org/08_info/Quotesf.html, accessed September 7, 2017. This quote is typically attributed to Mother Theresa, though it is not something she actually said. The author, then, is unknown.

3. http://izquotes.com/quote/193708, accessed September 7, 2017

4. http://www.azquotes.com/quote/543784, accessed September 7, 2017

5. http://proverbs14verse1.blogspot.com/2014/11/my-favorite-quotes-from-spurgeon.html, accessed September 7, 2017

6. http://www.inspirational-quotes-cafe.com/inspirational-quote-about-mother.html, accessed September 7, 2017

7. http://journaltimes.com/lifestyles/relationships-and-special-occasions/in-what-light-there-is-all-that-i-am/article_542bdbae-9492-11e1-961e-001a4bcf887a.html, accessed September 7, 2017

8. https://en.oxforddictionaries.com/definition/mundane, accessed September 7, 2017

9. Gloria Furman, *Treasuring Christ When Your Hands Are Full: Gospel Meditations for Busy Moms* (Wheaton, IL: Crossway, 2014) pg. 51

10. Ibid, pg. 51-52

11. Ibid, pg. 52-53

12. https://en.oxforddictionaries.com/definition/fulfilment, accessed September 7, 2017

13. http://www.hargraveshomeandhearth.com/011-the-work-at-home-mom-life-with-erika-oeding-hull/, accessed September 7, 2017

14. The bulk of this content originally appeared in a guest post I did for my friend, Sarah, on the topic of mommy guilt—http://www.christ
centeredmama.com/mommyguilt/, accessed August 12, 2017

15. http://www.hargraveshomeandhearth.com/011-dont-waste-your-wait-with-naomi-quick/, accessed September 8, 2017

16. https://www.blueletterbible.org/lang/lexicon/lexicon.cfm?Strongs=G5245&t=KJV, accessed September 8, 2017

17. Episode 11 of the Journeywomen Podcast—"Decorating and the Gospel", https://hunterbeless.com/new-blog/2017/7/23/ep11-on-
decorating-and-the-gospel, accessed September 8, 2017

18. http://www.theotherpages.org/poems/wallace1.html, accessed August 24th, 2017

19. Much of this portion originated in an article I wrote for my friend, Jenn—http://whatyoumakeitblog.com/2017/03/why-

we-feel-weak-in-our-marriages-and-mothering-guest-post-by-rebekah-hargraves.html, accessed September 11, 2017

20. Much of this portion originated in another article I wrote for Jenn—http://whatyoumakeitblog.com/2017/07/word-busy-wife-mama.html, accessed September 11, 2017

21. Much of this portion originated in an article I wrote for my friend, Lauren—http://www.chaoticlifeoflauren.com/2017/05/11/cultivating-creativity-motherhood/, accessed September 11, 2017

22. Much of this portion originated in an article I wrote for my friend, Amber—https://embracethisjoyfulllife.wordpress.com/2017/07/26/mama-you-are-too-busy-not-to-have-friends/, accessed September 11, 2017

23. http://www.biblestudytools.com/commentaries/matthew-henry-complete/proverbs/27.html, accessed September 11, 2017

24. As quoted in Michael A.G. Haykin, *8 Women of Faith* (Wheaton, IL: Crossway, 2016), pg. 99

25. Ibid, pg. 100

26. http://www.desiringgod.org/articles/motherhood-is-a-calling-and-where-your-children-rank, accessed August 24, 2017

27. http://money.cnn.com/2017/01/09/pf/cost-of-raising-a-child-2015/index.html, accessed August 29, 2017

28. See "At Home with Sally and Friends Episode 99: Convictions Come Through Table Talk"—http://sallyclarkson.com/podcast/2017/9/11/episode-99-convictions-come-through-table-

talk-with-sally-clarkson-and-kristen-kill, accessed September 18, 2017

29. See "God Centered Mom Podcast Episode 176: Gospel Parenting with Paul David Tripp"—http://godcenteredmom.com/2017/09/11/gospel-parenting-paul-david-tripp-ep-176/, accessed September 18, 2017

30. http://heavennotharvard.com/blog-posts/, accessed September 11, 2017

31. See https://www.gotquestions.org/Gamaliel-in-the-Bible.html, accessed September 11, 2017

32. https://www.goodreads.com/quotes/13915-freedom-is-never-more-than-one-generation-away-from-extinction, accessed August 30, 2017

33. See https://www.blueletterbible.org/lang/lexicon/lexicon.cfm?Strongs=G40&t=KJV and https://www.blueletterbible.org/lang/lexicon/lexicon.cfm?Strongs=G40&t=KJV, accessed September 11, 2017

Acknowledgements

Having read many a book in my time, I have seen several authors write that producing a book requires a multitude of people. I have now discovered for myself just how true that really is! An author alone is insufficient to the task of producing a good book—it truly takes a village of encouragers, helpers, and friends along the way to make the end result what it is.

And, for me, first and foremost it has taken my Lord and Savior, Jesus Christ. All glory and praise go to Him! I grew up hating writing, and I am certainly not one of those authors who always dreamed, from the time she was little, of being a writer. Rather, I'm an author who is flabbergasted to be so! The fact that I am now a writer simply reveals the miraculous work God can perform in His children (as well as His sense of humor!). Beyond this, however, I thank the Lord for also graciously working in such a miraculous way so as to make it possible for me to write a book with over 75,000 words in the span of one month! Apart from a small handful of pre-written blog articles, the bulk of this book was all new content. So, thank you, Lord, for having my little ones sleep so well in the mornings that I was able to write this book during that time and somehow still only take a month to do so. The prayer of my heart is that because of how You worked, readers would not be impressed with me, but be impressed with You. May they not praise me, but praise You. My hope is that they not thank me, but thank You for any good they find in this work. It truly is all thanks to You!

Secondly, major thanks goes to my sweet husband, Owen. Babe, you never think me crazy for having high and lofty writing dreams or for thinking up all these project ideas. You comfort me when I think I'm not good enough to be a writer, you cheer for me when I'm actually able to write something (and tell me how good what I wrote was!), and you share in my excitement when yet another new idea or opportunity comes my way. You truly are my biggest cheerleader, my partner in life, and my love. Thank you for being you, babe. I love you!

A huge, huge thank you also goes to my sweet mama! She did so much editing of the rough draft for me, and I am forever grateful! It pays to have what they call a "Grammar Nazi" as a mom! I love you so much, Mama, and am more blessed than you know to be your daughter (and not just because you're good at editing books!). I wouldn't be the woman, wife, and mama I am today were it not for you and the example you gave. The selfless work, unending love, and specific intention you put into raising and educating me on a daily basis can never be repaid, but I hope you know how much it has meant to me. I love you!

Additionally, anyone who writes-off the entire internet as being evil has not made the kind of online friends I have! Thank you so much to the ladies in the Conservative Christian Momma Bloggers Facebook group for your sweet support and excitement about this project!

Amber, you are a dear. You were probably the very first real friend I made online, and I am forever grateful to the Lord for causing our paths to cross. You are one of my biggest cheerleaders, and I can't thank you enough for the daily encouragement you send me via FB message. I love you to the moon and back, girl, and I'm still eagerly trying to find a way to get the state of Montana moved closer to Tennessee! Let me know if you find a solution to this problem we have!

Kayla, you have been my right-hand woman throughout the course of this project! And you are so stinkin' fun! Thank you for being just as excited about this book as I am and for brainstorming along with me all the things we could do in conjunction with the book itself (we wouldn't have mugs if it weren't for you!). Your joy, service, and selflessness are a blessing I could never begin to repay (plus, your downright hilarious GIFs on Facebook keep me in stitches!). Thank you for everything, not the least of which being the beautiful cover you so graciously and expertly designed for the book. You are talented, my friend!

Hannah, I've never met anyone quite like you. You run the powerhouse ministry that is the Young Wives Club, and yet you always take the time to ask me how you can serve me in my ministry. And you mean it! You don't just ask. You are always eager to find out how you can help and encourage me in what I'm doing and promote my work, and I thank the Lord for you. You are a true gift!

To all the ladies who contributed to this book by sharing with me the lies they have believed in motherhood—Marisa, Jenni, Vickie, Kayla, Suzanne, Caitlin, Amber, Charity, Hilary, Jenn, Michelle, Aileen, Selina, Gerri, Lauren Jane, Jessica, Brittany, Faith, Elizabeth, Chrissy, Phylicia, Summer, Laura, Natalie, Lena, Alice, Lisa, Sammie, Molly, Julia, Kathy, Brittany, Angela, Sheila, Sarah, Laura, Mary, Becca, Heather, Tami, and Esther—thank you for playing such an integral part in making this book what it is. It would not have been the same without your gracious willingness to share your heart and thoughts with me. God bless you!

My amazing, amazing launch team—Amber, Rebekah, Angela S., Angela P., Ali, Kayla, Hannah B., Victoria, Lauren, Angel, LauraJean, Hannah C., Tami, Kristen, Audrey, Tatiana, Kim, Marisa, Suzanne, April, both Amanda Cs.!, Starla, Esther, Tori, Summer R., Summer L., Betty, Joella, Faith, Sue, Lois, Cecy, Tania, Laura, Jessica A., Jessica H., Haley, Jill, Julie, Megan, Elizabeth, Erin, Brittany, Jenn, Sara, Michelle, and

Tamara—thank you from the bottom of my heart for being so willing to partner with me in getting the word out about this book. Y'all have blessed me more than you know, and it has been such fun and a true honor having you work alongside me in getting this project out there. #bestlaunchteamever!

To everyone who prayed for me throughout the course of writing this book—thank you! I'll never forget the day I started this project and was trying to figure out how I wanted my introduction to flow. I had so many ideas and couldn't, for the life of me, seem to find clarity for how it ought to be set up. I posted on Facebook that morning about my conundrum, asking for prayer, and, within minutes, I suddenly had inspiration and could barely type fast enough! It was the neatest thing. So, thank you!

And last, but certainly not least, thank you to my special Addi girl. I have been nannying you off and on since you were five weeks old and now, here you are, eight years old and such a big help to me in so many ways. Thank you for the amazing example you have always been to me of what having a servant's heart and always wanting to help people look like. You daily inspire me, sweet girl, through your constant question of, "Can I help?" Thank you for helping me on those days you kept an eye on the printer for me as the pages of the book came out for my mom to edit. You made sure the printer didn't jam up, and that's a hugely important job! Thank you for playing your own special part in the production of this book, and thank you for being a wonderful example to my own little girl of what it means to love others. I love you, Addi Pie!

LMB

About the Author

Rebekah Hargraves is a wife, mama to two littles, home business owner, blogger, and podcaster living in Tennessee. Though her primary passion is her family, she is also passionate about edifying, equipping, and encouraging women in their journey of Biblical womanhood. To that end, she runs the blog Hargraves Home and Hearth, produces the Home and Hearth podcast, and has now begun her writing career with her first book, *Lies Moms Believe.* When she isn't writing in the morning as her little ones sleep or keeping up with them the rest of the day, she also enjoys going on fun adventures with her husband, drinking copious amounts of hot tea and coffee, reading at least five books at once, and trying out new recipes! She can be found online at www.hargraveshomeandhearth.com, as well as on Facebook, Instagram, and Twitter.

Motherhood Is a Woman's Highest Calling *Mothering Is Unimportant Work* My Identity Is to Be Found in Being a Mother *I Am to Find My Ultimate Fulfillment in Motherhood* Mommy Guilt Is Just Something I Have to Live With *It's Wrong for Me to Go to God Again and Again After I Fail* Theology Isn't for Moms *I Have to Be a Perfect Mom* I Have to Do it All *I Am Enough* My Children Would Be Better Off Having a Different Mom *I'm a Bad Mom* I'm Selfish If I Have Any "Me Time" *I Need a Lot of "Me Time"* Motherhood Has to Be Hard (And Hard Is Bad!) *I Have to "Keep My Act Together"* I Can't Have a Clean House While Raising Children *My Life Is Passing Me By* *I Am Responsible for My Child's Happiness* I Can't Do This Whole "Mothering Thing" *My Success as a Mom Is Directly Tied to How My Children Turn Out* I Don't Know What It Means to Be a Mom If I Only Have One Child *I Don't Have Time* My Postpartum Body Has to Look a Certain Way *Children Are a Nuisance and an Interruption* Children Are Really Expensive *Children Ruin a Marriage* My Focus Should Be on Rules and Regulations *The "Experts" Know Better How to Raise and Educate My Child Than I Do* The Most Important Thing Is My Child's Education *Good Moms Do "XYZ"* You Have to "Do" Motherhood the Way the Culture Tells You

40553067R00166

Made in the USA
Middletown, DE
29 March 2019